PHILIPPIANS
and
COLOSSIANS

J. Vernon McGee

THOMAS NELSON PUBLISHERS

Nashville • Atlanta • London • Vancouver

Published in Nashville, Tennessee, by Thomas Nelson, Inc.

Scripture quotations are from the KING JAMES VERSION of the Bible.

Library of Congress Cataloging-in-Publication Data

McGee, J. Vernon (John Vernon), 1904–1988
   [Thru the Bible with J. Vernon McGee]
   Thru the Bible commentary series / J. Vernon McGee.
     p.   cm.
   Reprint. Originally published: Thru the Bible with J. Vernon McGee. 1975.
   Includes bibliographical references.
   ISBN 0-7852-1052-0 (TR)
   ISBN 0-7852-1110-1 (NRM)
   1. Bible—Commentaries. I. Title.
BS491.2.M37 1991
220.7′7—dc20   90–41340
                                 CIP

Printed in the United States of America

3 4 5 6 7 8 9 — 99 98 97 96 95

CONTENTS

PHILIPPIANS

COLOSSIANS

PREFACE

The radio broadcasts of the Thru the Bible Radio five-year program were transcribed, edited, and published first in single-volume paperbacks to accommodate the radio audience.

There has been a minimal amount of further editing for this publication. Therefore, these messages are not the word-for-word recording of the taped messages which went out over the air. The changes were necessary to accommodate a reading audience rather than a listening audience.

These are popular messages, prepared originally for a radio audience. They should not be considered a commentary on the entire Bible in any sense of that term. These messages are devoid of any attempt to present a theological or technical commentary on the Bible. Behind these messages is a great deal of research and study in order to interpret the Bible from a popular rather than from a scholarly (and too-often boring) viewpoint.

We have definitely and deliberately attempted "to put the cookies on the bottom shelf so that the kiddies could get them."

The fact that these messages have been translated into many languages for radio broadcasting and have been received with enthusiasm reveals the need for a simple teaching of the whole Bible for the masses of the world.

I am indebted to many people and to many sources for bringing this volume into existence. I should express my especial thanks to my secretary, Gertrude Cutler, who supervised the editorial work; to Dr. Elliott R. Cole, my associate, who handled all the detailed work with the publishers; and finally, to my wife Ruth for tenaciously encouraging me from the beginning to put my notes and messages into printed form.

Solomon wrote, ". . . of making many books there is no end; and much study is a weariness of the flesh" (Eccl. 12:12). On a sea of books that flood the marketplace, we launch this series of THRU THE BIBLE with the hope that it might draw many to the one Book, *The Bible.*

J. VERNON McGEE

PHILIPPIANS

The Epistle to the
PHILIPPIANS

INTRODUCTION

The Epistle of Paul to the Philippians is one of the Prison Epistles. Paul wrote four epistles when he was in prison, and we have labeled them Prison Epistles. They are Ephesians, Philippians, Colossians, and the little Epistle to Philemon.

The Epistle of Paul to the Philippians was written to the believers in Europe in the city of Philippi. This letter came out of a wonderful relationship that Paul had with the Philippian church. It seems that this church was closer to Paul than was any other church. Their love for him and his love for them are mirrored in this epistle. This epistle deals with Christian experience at the level on which all believers should be living. It is not a level on which all of us are, but it is where God wants us to be.

Paul visited Philippi on his second missionary journey. You will recall that he and Barnabas went on their first missionary journey to the Galatian country, where they had a wonderful ministry and founded many churches in spite of the persecution they encountered. Paul wanted to visit these churches on his second missionary journey. He wanted to take Barnabas with him again, but Barnabas insisted on taking his nephew, John Mark, who had been with them at the beginning of the first missionary journey. This young fellow, John Mark, you may remember, turned chicken and ran home to mama when they had landed on the coast of Asia Minor. Therefore, Paul did not want to take him the second time. So this split the team of Paul and Barnabas. Barnabas took John Mark and went in another direction. Paul, with

Silas for a companion, retraced his steps into the Galatian country, visiting the churches which they had established on the first missionary journey.

It would seem that Paul intended to widen his circle of missionary activity in that area, because a great population was there, and it was highly civilized. Actually, Greek culture and Greek learning were centered there at this particular time. Dr. Luke in recording it says that Paul attempted to go south into Asia, meaning the province of Asia, of which Ephesus was the leading city. But when he attempted to go south, the Spirit of God put up a roadblock. Since he wasn't to go south, Paul thought he would go north (where Turkey is today), but when ". . . they assayed to go into Bithynia . . . the Spirit suffered them not" (Acts 16:7).

Now he can't go south, he can't go north, he has come from the east, there is but one direction to go. So Paul went west as far as Troas. That was the end of the line. To go west of Troas he would have to go by boat. So Paul was waiting for instructions from God.

Sometimes we feel that God must lead us immediately, but God can let us wait. I think He lets us cool our heels many times, waiting for Him to lead us. If you are one who is fretting today, "Oh, what shall I do? Which way shall I turn?" Wait, just wait. If you are really walking with the Lord, He will lead you in His own good time.

So Paul continued to wait in the city of Troas (we know it as Troy) for orders, and he got them finally. He was given the vision of the man of Macedonia, recorded in Acts 16:9–10.

Paul and his companions boarded a ship that took them to the continent of Europe. To me this is the greatest crossing that ever has taken place because it took the gospel to Europe. I am thankful for that because at this particular time my ancestors were in Europe. One family was in the forests of Germany. I am told that they were as pagan and heathen as they possibly could have been. Another branch of the family was over in Scotland. And they, I am told, were the filthiest savages that ever have been on the topside of this earth. Now don't you look askance at me, because your ancestors were probably in the cave right next to my ancestors and they were just as dirty as mine were. I thank God today that the gospel went in that direction, because somewhere down the line some of these ancestors heard the Word of God, responded to it, and handed down to us a high type of civilization.

So Paul crossed over into Europe, and his first stop was Philippi. "And on the sabbath we went out of the city by a river side, where prayer was wont to be made; and we sat down, and spake unto the women which resorted thither. And a certain woman named Lydia, a seller of purple, of the city of Thyatira, which worshipped God, heard us: whose heart the Lord opened, that she attended unto the things which were spoken of Paul. And when she was baptized, and her household, she besought us, saying, If ye have judged me to be faithful to the Lord, come into my house, and abide there. And she constrained us" (Acts 16:13–15).

Paul, you see, found out that the man of Macedonia was a woman by the name of Lydia, holding a prayer meeting down by the river. That prayer meeting probably had a lot to do with bringing Paul to Europe. I'm of the opinion there were many people in Philippi who saw that group of women down there by the river praying and thought it wasn't very important. But it just happened to be responsible for the greatest crossing that ever took place! And Lydia was the first convert in Europe.

Now Lydia was a member of the Philippian church to which Paul wrote this epistle. We know something about some of the other members of this church also. There was a girl who was delivered from demon possession. "And it came to pass, as we went to prayer, a certain damsel possessed with a spirit of divination met us, which brought her masters much gain by soothsaying: The same followed Paul and us, and cried, saying, These men are the servants of the most high God, which shew unto us the way of salvation. And this did she many days. But Paul, being grieved, turned and said to the spirit, I command thee in the name of Jesus Christ to come out of her. And he came out the same hour" (Acts 16:16–18).

Also the Philippian jailer and his family were members of this church. You recall that Paul and Silas were thrown into jail at the instigation of the masters of the demon-possessed girl who had been deprived of their income. God intervened for Paul and Silas in such a miraculous way that their jailer came to know Christ. "And [the jailer] brought them out, and said, Sirs, what must I do to be saved? And they said, Believe on the Lord Jesus Christ, and thou shalt be saved, and thy house. . . . And when he had brought them into his house, he set meat before them, and rejoiced, believing in God with all his house" (Acts 16:30–31, 34).

There were, of course, other members of this Philippian church whose stories we do not know. They were a people very close to the apostle Paul. They followed him in his journeys and ministered to him time and time again. But when Paul was arrested in Jerusalem, they lost sight of him for two years. They did not know where he was. Finally they heard that he was in Rome in prison. The hearts of these people went out to him, and immediately they dispatched their pastor, Epaphroditus, with a gift that would minister to Paul's needs.

So Paul wrote this epistle to thank the church and to express his love for them. He had no doctrine to correct as he did in his Epistle to the Galatians. Neither did he have to correct their conduct, as he did in his Epistle to the Corinthians. There was only one small ripple in the fellowship of the church between two women, Euodias and Syntyche, and Paul gave them a word of admonishment near the end of his letter. He didn't seem to treat the matter as being serious.

His letter to the Philippian believers is the great epistle of Christian experience. This is Paul's subject in his epistle to the Philippians.

OUTLINE

I. Philosophy of Christian Living, Chapter 1
  A. Introduction, Chapter 1:1–2
  B. Paul's Tender Feeling for the Philippians, Chapter 1:3–11
  C. Bonds and Afflictions Further the Gospel, Chapter 1:12–20
  D. In Life or Death—Christ, Chapter 1:21–30

II. Pattern for Christian Living, Chapter 2
  A. Others, Chapter 2:1–4
  B. Mind of Christ—Humble, Chapter 2:5–8
  C. Mind of God—Exaltation of Christ, Chapter 2:9–11
  D. Mind of Paul—Things of Christ, Chapter 2:12–18
  E. Mind of Timothy—Like-minded with Paul, Chapter 2:19–24
  F. Mind of Epaphroditus—the Work of Christ, Chapter 2:25–30

III. Prize for Christian Living, Chapter 3
  A. Paul Changed His Bookkeeping System of the Past, Chapter 3:1–9
  B. Paul Changed His Purpose for the Present, Chapter 3:10–19
  C. Paul Changed His Hope for the Future, Chapter 3:20–21

IV. Power for Christian Living, Chapter 4
  A. Joy—the Source of Power, Chapter 4:1–4
  B. Prayer—the Secret of Power, Chapter 4:5–7
  C. Contemplation of Christ—the Sanctuary of Power, Chapter 4:8–9
  D. In Christ—the Satisfaction of Power, Chapter 4:10–23

CHAPTER 1

THEME: Philosophy of Christian living—Introduction; Paul's tender feeling for the Philippians; bonds and afflictions further the gospel; in life or death—Christ

Paul's letter to the Philippians is practical. It gets right down where we live. As we study this epistle, we won't be seated in the heavenlies as we were in his letter to the Ephesians, but we will be right down where the rubber meets the road. It is a wonderful little epistle, and we will be enriched by the sweetness of it.

INTRODUCTION

Paul and Timotheus, the servants of Jesus Christ, to all the saints in Christ Jesus which are at Philippi, with the bishops and deacons [Phil. 1:1].

"Paul and Timotheus"—Paul associates Timothy with himself. Paul brings this young preacher and puts him right beside himself, encouraging him. Paul loved this young man Timothy. He was Paul's son in the Lord, that is, he had won him to Christ; and Paul was very interested in him. Paul is constantly identifying certain young preachers with himself.

Now that I am getting old, I receive letters from former students and from many folk who in my ministry over the years have come to a knowledge of Christ. I feel that all of these are my children. I have a lot of children scattered around over this world, and I love them in the Lord. I understand how Paul felt about Timothy. Paul's name has come down through the centuries, and everywhere you hear about Paul, you will hear about Timothy—Paul was responsible for that. How wonderful!

"The servants of Jesus Christ." Paul identifies himself and Timothy as the servants of Jesus Christ. The word *servants* actually means "bondslaves." This is in contrast to his epistle to the Galatians where he was defending his apostleship. He began with, "Paul, an *apostle*." He did the same thing to the Corinthians. He had to declare and defend his apostleship and wanted them to know he was an apostle not *of* men, neither *by* man. He didn't need to defend himself with these Philippians. They loved him, and they accepted his apostleship. They had all been led to the Lord by him. So Paul takes a humble place, his rightful position: "Paul and Timotheus, we both are servants of the Lord Jesus Christ."

"To all the saints in Christ Jesus which are at Philippi." Paul is not writing to one little clique in the Philippian church; he is writing to all the saints, and every believer is a saint. The human family is divided into two groups: the saints and the ain'ts. Saints are believers in Christ. They are saints, not because of their conduct, but because of their position in Christ. *Saint* means "holy," set apart for God. Anything that is holy is separated for the use of God. Even the old pots and pans in the tabernacle were called "holy vessels," and they were probably beaten and battered after forty years in the wilderness. They may not have looked holy, but they were. Why? Because they had been set aside for the use of God. Now that should be the position of every child of God. We are set aside for the use of God. Now, friend, if you ain't a saint, then you are an ain't.

The saints are "in Christ Jesus." What does it mean to be saved? It means to be *in* Christ Jesus. When you put your trust in the Lord Jesus, the Spirit of God comes to dwell in you. The Holy Spirit baptizes you into the body of Christ. You are put in Christ by the Spirit of God.

Now these saints were *in* Christ, but they were *at* Philippi. You see, it doesn't make any difference where you are *at*—that may not be grammatically correct, but it is a true statement. You may be at Los Angeles or Duluth or Moscow or Philippi. It won't make any difference where you are *at*; the important matter is being *in* Christ Jesus.

I beieve the little phrase *in Christ* comprises the most important words that we have in the New Testament. What does it mean to be saved? I asked a theology professor that question, and he gave me quite a lecture on the subject. I was a little dizzy when he finished. He explained words like *propitiation* and *reconciliation* and *redemption*.

These are all marvelous words, and they are all Bible words, but not one of them covers the entire spectrum of salvation. The Spirit of God chose just one little word, the preposition *in*, to explain what salvation is. It is to be *in Christ*. How do you get in Christ? You get *in Christ* when you accept Him as your Savior.

"With the bishops and deacons." Notice he is addressing a local church with officers. "Bishop" means overseer or shepherd. The word *bishop* actually refers to the office, while the word *elder* refers to the individual who is in that office, and they should be men who are mature spiritually. "Deacons" refers to spiritual men who are performing a secular service (see Acts 6).

> **Grace be unto you, and peace, from God our Father, and from the Lord Jesus Christ [Phil. 1:2].**

"Grace be unto you, and peace." You will find this form of address in all of Paul's epistles, and grace and peace will always be in that sequence. Grace and peace were both commonplace words of Paul's day.

Grace was the word of greeting in the Greek world. In the Greek language it is *charis*. If you had walked down the street in that day, you would have heard folk greeting each other with, "Charis." In fact, this greeting is still used in modern Greece. It means grace. They say it as we say, "Have a good day." And God is saying to you, "Have a good eternity." When folk say to me, "Have a good day," they don't contribute anything to make it a good day other than just saying that. But God has made the arrangement whereby you can have a good eternity, and it is by the grace of God.

"Peace" always follows grace; it never precedes it. While *charis* comes out of the Greek world, "peace" *(shalom)* comes out of the religious world; it is the Hebrew form of greeting. Actually, the name *Jerusalem* means "the city of peace." Jeru-shalom—city of peace. It has never been that; it has been a city of war. Right now it is a thorn in the flesh of the world. No one knows what to do with it. There will never be peace in Jerusalem or in the world until the Prince of Peace comes to rule.

There is, however, a peace that comes to the believer through the grace of God. "Therefore being justified by faith, we have peace with God through our Lord Jesus Christ" (Rom. 5:1). This is the peace that a sinner can have with a holy God because Christ died for us, paid our penalty, and now God in His grace can save us. It is not that we bring God something for our salvation. Very frankly, we have nothing to bring to Him. I have never brought anything to Him—except sin. Christ paid the penalty for that sin so that a holy God can receive me. And He can receive you. In a world of turmoil, a world of tension, a world of trial, a world that is filled with things that are wrong, we can know the peace of God in our hearts. This is the peace of God that He gives to those who trust Jesus Christ as their own personal Savior. We must know the grace of God before we can experience the peace of God.

This grace and peace is "from God our Father, and from the Lord Jesus Christ." Let me ask this theological question: Isn't Paul a trinitarian? Doesn't he believe in the Trinity? Then why doesn't he include the Holy Spirit with the Father and the Son? The reason is that the Holy Spirit is already over there in Philippi, indwelling the believers. Certainly Paul believed in the Trinity: Father, Son, and Holy Spirit; and he is being very accurate here.

PAUL'S TENDER FEELING FOR THE PHILIPPIANS

I thank my God upon every remembrance of you [Phil. 1:3].

He begins the body of his letter in this very lovely manner, which reveals the sweet relationship between Paul and the Philippian believers. That is the way it ought to be today among believers, especially between pastor and congregation. The literal translation would be, "All my remembrance of you causes me to thank God." Every time anybody would mention Philippi, Paul would just thank God for the believers there. That is something really quite wonderful.

Every now and then I get a letter from some organization that wants me to do something for them. That is perfectly legitimate for them to make such a request, but they begin the letter with, "I thank my God upon every remembrance of you." Sometimes I'm not so sure they really feel that way about me, but they are preparing me for the request that is coming. But how wonderful it would be to have a church like the Philippian church. And how wonderful to be the kind of person about which it can be said, "All my remembrance of you causes me to thank God." If Paul hadn't said anything else about his relationship to this church, this would have been enough to reveal how special it was. You can check the other epistles—he didn't say this to the other churches, certainly not about the Galatians or the Corinthians.

> **Always in every prayer of mine for you all making request with joy [Phil. 1:4].**

"Always"—not just sometimes. Always in every prayer Paul remembered the Philippian believers.

The phrase "for you all" makes it very clear that Paul was speaking to all the saints that were in that church, the corporate body in the local church. When we reach the final chapter of this epistle, we will find that there was a little ripple of discord between two women in the Philippian church: Snytyche and Euodias. So Paul at the very beginning was careful to include all the saints in order that one group couldn't say to the other, "He is writing to us and not to you."

"Making request with joy." Bengel said that the sum of this epistle is: "I rejoice; rejoice ye." We realize what a remarkable expression this is when we consider where Paul was when he wrote. He was over in Rome in prison! He probably was not in the Mamertine prison at this time, but he was in a place equally as disagreeable.

Although the word *joy* appears nineteen times in this epistle, I have never felt that it should be called the "joy epistle." If we are going to pick out the word that occurs more than any other word, we must take the name of Jesus Christ. His name appears over forty times in this epistle. He is the center of the epistle. He is the One who is the very source of joy. Therefore, the emphasis should be put upon Him rather than upon the joy. As we shall see, the *philosophy* of Christian living has to do with Him; the *pattern* has to do with Him. The *price* of Christian living has to do with Him, and the *power* has to do with

Him. Actually, it is a personal relationship with Christ that brings joy to a believer's life.

We try to produce joy in the church by external means. We have a program and tell folks, "Come and you will enjoy it." We have a banquet—people enjoy a banquet—so we have joy, we say. Actually, joy does not depend upon outward circumstances. Real joy depends upon the inward condition of the individual. It depends on the proper attitude toward life. If you are complaining and whining about your lot in life, certainly you will not be experiencing joy. You may be able to go to a church banquet and have a little fun, but that will not be joy. When you and I get to the place where we find ourselves in the center of the will of God and know we are in His will regardless of our circumstances, then there will be joy in our lives.

Paul said, "Always in every prayer of mine for you all making request with joy." The time of prayer was not an ordeal for Paul. He didn't say *Oh, I've got to go through the ordeal of praying for those folk again!* No. He said, "As I am here in jail, it is a lot of fun to pray for you Philippians; it brings joy to my heart."

Now, having told them he thanked God for them, he gives a reason.

For your fellowship in the gospel from the first day until now [Phil. 1:5].

"For your fellowship in the gospel." Now we have come to a very important word in this epistle. We do not want to pass over this word *fellowship*. This word is used widely in the church and outside the church. I don't think that most people really know what the word means, and therefore they don't use it properly.

Years ago I was invited down to Huntington Beach about once a year to give a message at a Rotary Club luncheon. A Christian doctor was chairman of the program committee down there, and he would invite me to come at Christmastime or Eastertime and give them the gospel—both barrels, which is what I always tried to do.

Over the speaker's table they had a slogan: "Food, Fun, Fellowship." Those three things belonged to the early church, and I didn't feel that the Rotary Club should have bragged about having any one of the three. For food there would be embalmed chicken with peas as hard as bullets. For fun they had corny jokes. The fellowship consisted of patting someone on the back and saying, "Hello, Bill. How's business?"

Now that is not fellowship in the biblical sense of the word. The Greek word is koinōnia, and it means that which believers can share of the things of Christ. There are three elements that must enter into it: spiritual communication, sympathetic cooperation, and sweet communion. (1) Spiritual communication is sharing the things of Christ. This would be sharing the great truths concerning Christ. (2) Sympathetic cooperation means working together for Christ. That is why, when Paul used the word *fellowship,* he could be talking about Bible reading or Bible study together or prayer or celebrating the Lord's Supper or taking up an offering. Paul called all of these koinōnia—fellowship. The result would be (3) sweet communion. It makes us partners with Christ. This is true koinōnia.

Paul wrote that this church was having fellowship with him. He had communicated to them the gospel. They had shared with Paul in a sympathetic cooperation. They had sent a gift to him and had ministered to his physical needs again and again. Then when they were together, they had sweet communion.

"From the first day until now"—Paul had enjoyed wonderful fellowship with them from the first day, that day he had met Lydia and her group praying by the riverside.

Being confident of this very thing, that he which hath begun a good work in you will perform it until the day of Jesus Christ [Phil. 1:6].

Because this is my life verse and therefore very meaningful to me, I hope you won't mind if I tell you about it. I was a very poor boy when I went away to college. My dad had been killed in an accident in a cotton gin when I was fourteen years old. My mother took my sister and me to Nashville, Tennessee. I had to get a permit that allowed a boy of fourteen to go to work, and I worked for a wholesale hardware concern. I had to be up by five o'clock in the morning to pick up the mail and have it sorted and on the desks of all the officials in each department. I should have been in school, and I wanted to go to school. Later I had the privilege of going back to school because a wonderful friend acted as a father to me. He had a son who was a drunkard. He had wanted his son to get a college education, but he didn't; so the man helped me get a job, and I was able to go to college. Every year I thought it would be my last year. I never thought God would see me through—I had very little faith. The last year I was in college was during the depression; 1928 and 1929 were bad years. I couldn't get a job and had no money.

On graduation day, after receiving my degree, I returned to my room in the dormitory, still in my cap and gown, and sat dejectedly on the edge of my bed. My roommate came and asked, "What in the world—did somebody die?" I said, "Just as well to. I thought God had called me to the ministry. I'm through college, the depression has hit, and I don't even have a job for this summer. I haven't a dime to go to seminary next year." While we were still talking, the phone rang. It was for me. On the other end of the line was a dear little lady who asked me to stop by her home where she lived with her sister. They were both widows, and they looked as if they had come out of the antebellum days. They attended the church where I taught a class of intermediate boys, and I herded the boys into the church service every Sunday morning. The sisters sat in the pew behind us, and I always thought they disapproved. But in their home that day each handed me an envelope in memory of her husband. I left as soon as it was polite to go, hurried around the corner, and opened the envelopes. The first contained a check for $250; I hurriedly opened the other envelope and found another check for $250. Do you know what $500 was like during the depression? I felt like a millionaire!

That night the Sunday school had a banquet for me, a farewell banquet, and they gave me a check for $100. So now I had $600! That is the money with which I went to seminary the next year. That night at the banquet someone gave me this verse: "Being confident of this very thing, that he which hath begun a good work in you will perform it until the day of Jesus Christ." That has been my life verse ever since that night.

Now let's consider this verse for a moment.

"Being confident" is causative and could be translated, "*Since* I am confident of this very thing"—Paul knew what he was talking about.

"He which hath begun . . . will perform." The word for "perform" means to carry through. He will consummate what He began.

"Until the day of Jesus Christ." You and I today are not living in the Day of the Lord; we are not living in the day of the Old Testament; we are not living in the day of the Millennium; we are not living in the day of eternity; we are living in the day of Jesus Christ. That day will be consummated when He comes to take His own out of this world. And the Holy Spirit has sealed you and me until the day of redemption. Paul wrote to the Ephesian believers, "And grieve not the Holy Spirit of God, whereby ye are sealed unto the day of redemption" (Eph. 4:30). And until then, you can count upon God to consummate whatever He intends for you. He is going to see it through. How wonderful!

Now, my friend, let me ask you this: Is this practical for you and me? I don't know what your circumstances are, but if you are a child of God, I am sure you can testify that God has brought you up to the present moment, hasn't He? Can't you look back over your life and see how He has led you and provided for you? Then why should you be concerned about tomorrow? Do you think He is going to let you down now? I confess that this was my thinking when I finished college.

You see, I went through college, but I didn't enjoy it as I should have. I never had joy because I always was afraid I couldn't go on. I just didn't believe God would see me through. So many times we Christians act like unbelievers. In fact, we live and act like practical atheists. The graduation was a happy experience for my classmates. I could see those rich kids being hugged by their parents. No one was there to throw their arms around me, but it wouldn't have made any difference if there had been a whole delegation of well-wishers, because I thought I was through. I felt called to the ministry, but there was no possible way for me to go on to seminary. However, I had a wonderful heavenly Father who, through Philippians 1:6, put His arms around me and said, "I'll see you through."

And I want to testify today that He is still keeping His promise. It has been a comfort to me since I have had several bouts with cancer to know that my heavenly Father said, "Being confident of this very thing, that he which hath begun a good work in you will perform it until the day of Jesus Christ." He is a good Doctor also; in fact, He is the Great Physician, and He has said, "Whatever I have in store for you, I'm going to see you through until the day of Jesus Christ." So I am in His hands.

This is a great verse of Scripture. Oh, I have held onto this during many a dark night when the storm outside was beating against my little bark. My, how wonderful to have a heavenly Father like this!

> **Even as it is meet for me to think this of you all, because I have you in my heart; inasmuch as both in my bonds, and in the defence and confirmation of the gospel, ye all are partakers of my grace [Phil. 1:7].**

"Even as it is meet"—*meet* is an old Elizabethan word that means "right." Even as it is right for me to think this of you all.

"Because I have you in my heart." Isn't that a wonderful place to carry your Christian friends?

"Partakers of my grace" brings us back to the word *fellowship*. It is *koinōnia* with a preposition that intensifies it: *suqkoinōnous*, meaning "being all wrapped up together." You may remember that lovely Abigail used these words when she talked to David: ". . . but the soul of my lord shall be bound in the bundle of life with the LORD thy God . . ." (1 Sam. 25:29). Paul is saying that he and the Philippians are all wrapped up together as partners in the gospel.

This is what I mean when I say that there were tender feelings of the apostle Paul for this church at Philippi. He was closer to them than to any other church. It is so wonderful to have Christian friends like this who are sharing in the great enterprise of getting out the Word of God. There is that sympathetic cooperation, besides the spiritual communication, and it always produces sweet communion.

> **For God is my record, how greatly I long after you all in the bowels of Jesus Christ [Phil. 1:8].**

That word *bowels* is offensive to some folk. One sweet little lady, who

I'm sure had never used a bad word in her life, came to me and said, "Dr. McGee, don't read it like that. That's crude." I answered, "That's the way it is in the Bible, and that's the way I think it should be read—just as it is." *Bowels* really means tender feelings. This is really a marvelous statement. Paul says that he longs for all of them in the tender feelings of Jesus Christ. Actually, it is quite accurate to use the word *bowels* for tender feelings.

I was teaching this one night at Bible study, and at that time a psychologist from the University of Southern California attended the classes. I was teaching that bowels meant tender feelings. He said, "The ancients were right. They were accurate when they talked about our feelings being in the region of the bowels." He said, "The average person thinks that everything he does is because he has thought it over and that he is very smart." Then he touched me on the head and said, "Very little really takes place up here." I really felt that he knew me when he said that.

He went on to explain that the brain is really a very marvelous telephone exchange. A message comes up through the sensory nervous system, up through the synaptical connections from the hand to the brain. Immediately there is a transfer made over to a motor neuron, and the message goes down over a different set of synaptical connections. For example, when you touch a hot stove, immediately the message goes up to the brain, and the brain returns the message, "Take your finger off that—you'll get burned." You react instantly. You do it without thinking, but there was a connection made up in the brain. By the way, many people drive an automobile like that—without thinking, which is quite obvious. Then he asked me, "How did you feel the first time you saw your wife? Where did that take place? Was it in the brain?" The psychologist points to my tummy and said, "There is where you live and move and have your being." So Paul is expressing his most tender feelings, "I long after you." It is not because they have given him something. His reaction is not mental but emotional. This is a wonderful expression.

And this I pray, that your love may abound yet more and more in knowledge and in all judgment [Phil. 1:9].

There is a lot of silly thinking about this word *love*. I often get letters such as this one: "You gave me the surprise of my life when you said that there are certain preachers who spread damnable heresies. Doesn't Jesus say in His Holy Word that we are to love our enemies and do good to those who hate us?" Of course He said that, but we need to notice to whom he said it. The Lord Jesus had some very harsh things to say about the religious rulers of His day. He said, "Ye are of your father the devil, and the lusts of your father ye will do . . ." (John 8:44). Also He said, "Ye serpents, ye generation of vipers, how can ye escape the damnation of hell?" (Matt. 23:33). He called the Devil their father and a snake their mother! I don't think any person could be more extreme.

Paul prays that your "love may abound yet more and more in knowledge and in all judgment [or *discernment*]." We are to love all believers in Christ. Some of the believers are a little difficult to love. Some of our friends are even difficult to love. We are to love the unlovely, but we are to love with knowledge and with discernment. That does not mean we just let our love slop over on every side. It is to abound with discernment. Let me give you an illustration out of my own experience.

When I first went to downtown Los Angeles as a pastor, I soon found that there are certain groups that move through that downtown area and prey on church people and new preachers especially. One Sunday morning one of the personal workers came to me and said, "There's a man here who has come forward and wants to talk to you about his salvation." Well, I felt complimented. This man wants to talk to me; he won't talk to anybody else. So I went over to talk to him, and by that time practically everybody had left the church. I began to explain the plan of salvation. I never saw a fellow so interested. He took my Bible and read the verses I indicated. Oh, he had it down to a system! Finally I asked him if he wanted to accept Christ. Tears came to his eyes and ran down his face. He said yes, he did. We got down on our knees, and he prayed. When we stood up, I made a mistake. I asked him how he was getting along. And he told me, "I hate to tell you this, but my suitcase is down here in a certain hotel. They won't let me have it because I owe them seven dollars." Well, what would you do? You had just led a man to the Lord, supposedly; you're a Christian; you're a preacher; you ought to love the brother. Well, I gave him the seven dollars, and I felt expansive. I told my wife about it and felt very good inside that I had been so generous. About six weeks after that I was going through the daily paper, and there was a picture of this man. I thought, *How in the world did he get into the paper?* And I read that he'd been arrested. He had spent the previous six months in Los Angeles living off the preachers, and his comment was, "They are the biggest saps in the world." And I was one of them! I called up the late Dr. Bob Schuler, who was pastoring in downtown Los Angeles at Trinity Methodist Church, and asked, "Did this fellow come down to you?" "Yes," he said. "Did you let him have seven dollars?" He said, "No. That's what he wanted, but I've been down here a long time, Vernon. After you've been down here awhile, you'll find there are some you can't love."

Paul says to let your love abound more and more, but let it abound in judgment, let it abound in being able to discern. Over the years when I would drive to my study in Los Angeles, I used to say to the Lord, "I'm going to meet new people today, and I don't know them. Some of them I'll be able to help. Others of them will put a knife in my back. Lord, help me to be able to distinguish between the two. Show me which I should help." Actually this verse rescues a Christian from being naive and gullible. His love is to abound in knowledge and discernment.

That ye may approve things that are excellent; that ye may be sincere and without offence till the day of Christ [Phil. 1:10].

Here is another important verse that needs some explanation. When Paul says, "That ye may approve things that are excellent," he means that you need to try the things that differ. This has to do, I believe, with the Lord's will for your life. There are times when we must come to a decision when there are two or more routes that we could go. What one shall we take? Frankly, there are times when we don't know. The Lord will not send an angel to tell us, nor will He turn on red or green lights to give us signals. He expects us to use a little consecrated and concentrated gumption. Therefore we need to try the things that differ.

A man was telling me about his business. He had two routes open to him, and he prayed about his decision. He tried one of them, and it didn't work. He told me that when he saw it wouldn't work, he came back to the crossroads and tried the other route. He said, "Then I was sure of the Lord's will. The one route didn't work, so there was only one other way open for me. I followed that one, and it was the right one." God says we are to try the things that differ. Actually, that is the way He leads us.

"That ye may be sincere"—"sincere" is an interesting word which comes from the Latin *sincerus*, which means without wax. When the Romans became a world power, they were a very strong and rather brutal people. They destroyed a great many of the art treasures of Greece in many places. In the cities of Asia Minor, we can still see evidence of that. I was interested in looking at several of the temples over there; the temple of Diana must have been a beautiful thing from the architectural standpoint. But many of the art troves of Greece were broken up. When the Romans reached the point of development in their culture that they appreciated these things, they began to gather them up. Many of them were broken. When there was a crack in a statute or a vase, a dishonest dealer would fill it in with wax so that one couldn't tell that it had been broken. Then he would sell it as a genuine, perfect piece. An unsuspecting man would buy it, take it to his villa, and display it in his garden. The next hot day he would walk out and, lo and behold, the wax would be running out of a crack in that lovely art treasure! Finally the reputable art dealers began to put on their material the word *sincerus*, meaning without wax. In other words, they guaranteed it was a perfect piece.

Paul is saying, "Don't be a phony. Be real, be genuine, be sincere." Applying this to the previous verse, don't go around patting everyone on the back with a "Praise the Lord, Hallelujah" and telling them how much you love them if you are going to stick a knife in their backs the minute they leave your presence. That is what he is saying here. Be sincere.

"Without offence" means *blameless*, which would be a better translation, because we cannot live the Christian life or preach the Word of God without offense to somebody. Remember that people were offended at Paul and his preaching. That is the reason believers should pray for their pastor if he is preaching the Bible. If he is really giving out the Word of God, there will be offense. He needs your support, your defense of him, your prayers for him.

I officiated at a funeral service for a movie star several years ago. I preached the Word of God, and the crowd attending the service didn't appreciate what I said. They were antagonistic. I even got some telephone calls from some of the people. One of the television newscasters gave the report of the funeral and said, "Hollywood heard something today that they have never heard before"—I understand he was a Christian. But my message was an offense to most of that crowd. So you see, the Christian life and the preaching of the Word of God will not be without offense to someone, but Paul is saying that believers should be *blameless*.

When I first became pastor in downtown Los Angeles, I met Dr. Jim McGinnis who was in Chicago at that time. He asked me how I liked being a pastor in downtown Los Angeles. I said, "Well, I certainly am enjoying it. It is a marvelous opportunity, and the crowds are coming to church, but I find I can't defend myself. I hear reports about me that are terrible." He answered, "That's all right. Just be sure that none of them are true." We can be blameless, but we cannot be without offense.

"Till the day of Christ" has reference to His coming for His own. This is the second time the Rapture is mentioned in this epistle. A child of God should walk in the light of the imminent return of Christ all the time.

Being filled with the fruits of righteousness, which are by Jesus Christ, unto the glory and praise of God [Phil. 1:11].

The "fruits of righteousness" are the fruits of the Holy Spirit. The Holy Spirit is producing fruit in the lives of the believers. ". . . The fruit of the Spirit is love, joy, peace, longsuffering, gentleness, goodness, faith, meekness, temperance . . ." (Gal. 5:22–23).

BONDS AND AFFLICTIONS FURTHER THE GOSPEL

But I would ye should understand, brethren, that the things which happened unto me have fallen out rather unto the furtherance of the gospel [Phil. 1:12].

Paul is speaking very emphatically to them. When the believers in Philippi heard that Paul was in prison, they sent a message to him by their pastor, Epaphroditus, and it probably went something like this: "Oh, poor brother Paul, we feel so sorry for you. Now your great missionary journeys are curtailed; you are in prison, and the gospel is not going out!" Paul said, "Look, I want you to know that the gospel is going out, and the things that have happened to me have not curtailed but have actually furthered the gospel."

Now he will make clear what he means by this.

So that my bonds in Christ are manifest in all the palace, and in all other places [Phil. 1:13].

The palace was actually Caesar's court. Acts 28:16 tells us, "And when we came to Rome, the centurion delivered the prisoners to the captain of the guard: but Paul was suffered to dwell by himself with a soldier that kept him." Paul was chained to a member of the Praetorian Guard, and these men were the Roman patricians, members of Caesar's household.

When Paul was converted, the Lord Jesus said that Paul would ". . . bear my name before the Gentiles, and kings, and the children of Israel" (Acts 9:15). Well, up to this time Paul had taken the gospel largely to the common, vegetable variety of citizens in the Roman Empire. But now he has members of the royalty chained to him! Every four hours, at the change of the guard, one guard would leave and be replaced by a new guard who would be chained to Paul. What do you think Paul talked about during those four hours? Can you imagine having your congregation chained to you? My guess is that some of them were happy to see their relief guard come. They would say, "Boy, am I glad to see you! This man Paul is trying to make a Christian out of me." Many of them did come to know Christ. The gospel penetrated Caesar's household. Later Tertullian wrote that the Roman government became disturbed when it was discovered that Christians were in positions of authority. Many of these men later died for their faith in the Lord Jesus Christ.

This is the first evidence Paul gave that his imprisonment had not hindered the furtherance of the gospel but that it had enabled him to bring the gospel right into Caesar's household.

Not only did Paul's imprisonment enable him to reach into Caesar's household with the gospel, but it also accomplished something else:

And many of the brethren in the Lord, waxing confident by my bonds, are much more bold to speak the word without fear [Phil. 1:14].

In the early church there were many men who were willing to go out as witnesses for Christ, but after hearing Paul speak, they would say something like this, "Man, I'd like to witness for the Lord, but I can't tell it like Paul tells it." So long as Paul was out preaching the gospel, others would feel unworthy, not competent or sufficiently trained. They considered Paul so much more effective than they could be. But then one day the word went down the Roman roads to all those centers where churches had been established that Paul was in prison in Rome. In many of those churches men would say, "Look, Paul's in prison. He can't go out anymore. I'll go." As a result many men started to preach the gospel. I am confident that hundreds and maybe even thousands of men hit the Roman roads and moved out from door to door to tell people about Christ. So Paul says, "Many of the brethren in the Lord, waxing confident by my bonds, are much more bold to speak the word without fear."

Now I believe there is a third effect of Paul's imprisonment which he does not mention. We can only get this from the perspective of history. Paul may not have realized the importance of his writing, but if he had not been put into prison, we would not have the Prison Epistles: Ephesians, Philippians, Colossians, Philemon. They are all marvelous epistles, and we would not have them today if Paul had not been in prison. I'm sure the Lord could have gotten this teaching to us some other way, but this was the way He chose. So Paul could say about his imprisonment that it had "fallen out rather unto the furtherance of the gospel."

There was, however, a tragic difficulty in Paul's day. We have the same thing happening in this day, and it is still tragic.

Some indeed preach Christ even of envy and strife; and some also of good will [Phil. 1:15].

When I first began to study the Bible, it was unbelievable to me that the preaching of the gospel of Christ could be done in envy and strife. But now that I've been in the ministry for a long time—I was ordained in 1933—I know that one of the things that hurts the preaching of the gospel probably more than any other single thing is the envy and the strife. Paul will mention envy and strife several times in this epistle. There must have been quite a few who were preaching the gospel in that way, envious of the apostle Paul, jealous because they didn't have the results that Paul had.

One of the solutions to this problem of envy is for every Christian to recognize that he has a gift. We do not all have the same gift. The body could not function if we did. The problem is that some men who have one gift are envious of a man who has a different gift. You will remember that Paul told the Corinthians that the gifts are to be exercised in love. Every gift is to be exercised in love. My friend, if you will exercise your gift in love, you will not envy someone else. ". . . Love envieth not; love vaunteth not itself, is not puffed up" (1 Cor. 13:4). Envy says, "I don't think much of you," and pride says, "What do you think of me?" That is the difference between envy and pride, and the believer is warned against both of them. Paul put it very bluntly when he wrote, "For who maketh thee to differ from another? and what hast thou that thou didst not receive? now if thou didst receive it, why dost thou glory, as if thou hadst not received it?" (1 Cor. 4:7).

Strife is an interesting word. It is the Greek word *eris*, which means "to stir up"—referring to demons, the spirits, that stir up strife. Envy and strife! Those two still hurt the church. Alcohol and drugs on the outside of the church cannot hurt it nearly as much as the envy and strife on the inside of the church.

Notice, however, that there were some who preached Christ of good will.

> **The one preach Christ of contention, not sincerely, supposing to add affliction to my bonds [Phil. 1:16].**

Those motivated by envy and strife preached Christ, but not sincerely. They actually did it to try to belittle Paul. They were envious of the apostle Paul, but they had not been able to say anything against him. Now that he was in prison and unable to defend himself, these men would go out and preach the gospel, but they also would have a few little things to say against Paul.

> **But the other of love, knowing that I am set for the defence of the gospel [Phil. 1:17].**

These are the two groups. What is Paul's attitude toward them?

> **What then? notwithstanding, every way, whether in pretence, or in truth, Christ is preached; and I therein do rejoice, yea, and will rejoice [Phil. 1:18].**

The important thing to Paul was that Christ be preached, no matter whether it was done in pretense or by true motives. It is tragic that at times Christ is preached in envy and strife. He is still preached in that way today, but we can always rejoice whenever Christ is preached.

I am a little rough on female preachers because I believe they are unscriptural, but, as I have said on several occasions, some women are preaching Christ better than the average male preacher. What is my position? I *rejoice* and thank God that Christ is being preached.

Dr. Ironside told the story of walking through a park in Oakland,

California. A woman was preaching there, and his friend said to him, "Isn't it a shame that this woman is here preaching?" Dr. Ironside said, "It's a shame that there is not some man to take her place." That is the problem. Thank God, Christ is being preached. That is the important thing. We can rejoice today whenever the Word of God is given out.

At the time I am writing, a great many folk are getting concerned about home Bible classes. I am *rejoicing* over them. I know sometimes they go off on a tangent, but not any more than some churches go off on tangents. We can rejoice that the Word of God is being taught.

It is interesting and also comforting to know that Christ can be preached insincerely, and yet people can still be saved. God honors His Word, not the man or the organization. We need to recognize that today. The Spirit of God is the *only* One who can bring blessings, and He can bless *only* when the Word of God is given out.

For I know that this shall turn to my salvation through your prayer, and the supply of the Spirit of Jesus Christ [Phil. 1:19].

By the word *salvation* Paul means his deliverance from prison.

"Through your prayer." People have asked me why I asked everyone to pray for me when I had cancer. They said, "Didn't you know that God would heal you if you go to Him in prayer?" May I say that the Bible makes it clear that God hears and answers the prayers of His people. We need to ask God's people to pray for us. Paul says that through their prayers he hopes to be set free.

"Through . . . the supply of the Spirit of Jesus Christ." The only way you and I can get that supply that we need is through prayer.

According to my earnest expectation and my hope, that in nothing I shall be ashamed, but that with all boldness, as always, so now also Christ shall be magnified in my body, whether it be by life, or by death [Phil. 1:20].

Paul said he did not want to be ashamed of his witness while in this life, and he did not want to be ashamed when he came into the presence of the Lord Jesus Christ. The apostle John mentions the fact that when Christ comes to take His church with Him, it is possible for believers to be ashamed at His appearing (see 1 John 2:28). We need to bear that in mind. All Christians ought to be concerned about that.

Years ago I began a prophetic congress in downtown Los Angeles which has spread over this entire area and has given a tremendous emphasis to prophecy. This has been carried out across our country today. I probably have spoken in more prophetic congresses than any one individual. So I want to say this: there are too many people who are talking about the coming of the Lord but are not ready for the coming of the Lord. You may ask, "Aren't they saved?" Yes, they are saved. But I'm afraid they will be ashamed at His appearing. Their lives do not commend the gospel. Paul says that he doesn't want to be ashamed before Christ at His coming.

You will recall that this chapter gives the philosophy of Christian living. You will find that Paul will sum up the theme of each of these four chapters in one verse, and sometimes in one sentence. The next verse puts this chapter in a nutshell.

IN LIFE OR DEATH—CHRIST

For to me to live is Christ, and to die is gain [Phil. 1:21].

Notice in your Bible that the verb *is* is in italics. That means it is not in the original but had been added to make the meaning clearer. The verse is actually, "For to me to live Christ, and to die gain."

This is the philosophy of Christian living: To live Christ; to die gain. Dr. William L. Pettingill used to say that *gain* is always more of the same thing. If to live is Christ, then to die would be more of Christ. It means to go and be with Him.

Although it has taken me a long time to arrive at this conclusion, I am convinced that the most important thing in my life as a Christian is to have the reality of Jesus Christ in my life. This is not too popular today. People would rather talk about being dedicated, wanting to

serve Him, or doing this and that. But the most important thing is to
have fellowship with Him so that your joy might be full. Then we will
have a powerful witness. The problem is that most people want the
end but forget all about the means. The means, in this case, is fellowship with the Lord Jesus Christ. Everything else is the fruitage of this
fellowship. For me to live is Christ; to die is to be with Him.

Now we know why Paul was undisturbed by the criticism being
leveled at him. You can't hurt a man who is in fellowship with Jesus
Christ. What could anyone do to such a man? "For to me to live
Christ, and to die gain" is a high plane on which to live. I wish I could
say I have reached that plane. I'm on my way, and I haven't arrived,
but that is my *goal*. What a glorious one it is!

> **But if I live in the flesh, this is the fruit of my labour: yet
> what I shall choose I wot not [Phil. 1:22].**

Paul didn't know about his future, just as you and I don't know about
our future. We don't know what any single day will bring forth.

> **For I am in a strait betwixt two, having a desire to de-
> part, and to be with Christ; which is far better:**
>
> **Nevertheless to abide in the flesh is more needful for you
> [Phil. 1:23–24].**

Paul says he was torn between wanting to go to be with the Lord,
which is the better of the two, or staying with the Philippian believers
because they needed him.

The first time I had cancer surgery, a letter came from a lady that
said, "I know that everybody is praying that you will get well, but I
am praying that the Lord will take you home because to be with Christ
is far better." I wrote back and said, "Would you mind letting the Lord
decide about this? I want to stay." I want to stay a while longer to give
out the Word of God. I've just now gotten to the best part of my ministry, and I don't want to leave it. I'm asking God to let me stay with it. I
think that is a normal feeling for a child of God.

It reminds me of a story of an incident that took place in my south-land in a black church. The preacher asked one night, "How many of you want to go to heaven?" Everyone put up his hand except one little boy. The preacher asked him, "Don't you want to go to heaven?" He answered, "I sure do, but I thought you were getting up a load for tonight."

We all want to go to heaven, but not *right now!*

> **And having this confidence, I know that I shall abide and continue with you all for your furtherance and joy of faith;**
>
> **That your rejoicing may be more abundant in Jesus Christ for me by my coming to you again [Phil. 1:25–26].**

Paul is practical. He still has work to do. These folk need his ministry. He wanted to get out of prison and go to be with them again.

People who are always saying, "Oh, if the Lord would only come," should get busy. This is the only place where we can do any work that is going to count for a reward for Him. This is the stage on which you and I play our part. I want to stay as long as possible, and I have promised the Lord I will teach the Word as long as He lets me stay.

> **Only let your conversation be as it becometh the gospel of Christ: that whether I come and see you, or else be absent, I may hear of your affairs, that ye stand fast in one spirit, with one mind striving together for the faith of the gospel [Phil. 1:27].**

The word *conversation* means your way of life. Not only our speech but our entire way of life should be a credit to the gospel of Christ.

"Stand fast in one spirit, with one mind striving together for the faith of the gospel"—oh, how God's people need to stand together for the furtherance of the gospel! If the church were what it should be in the world today, the world would listen to the message it proclaims.

Here Paul uses the word *strive* which is so different from the word *strife* about which he wrote earlier in the chapter. In the word *strive* is the thought of agonizing. We are to agonize together for the faith of the gospel.

> **And in nothing terrified by your adversaries: which is to them an evident token of perdition, but to you of salvation, and that of God.**

> **For unto you it is given in the behalf of Christ, not only to believe on him, but also to suffer for his sake [Phil. 1:28–29].**

When you get to the place where He lets you suffer for Him, you have arrived—that is the high calling of Christ Jesus.

> **Having the same conflict which ye saw in me, and now hear to be in me [Phil. 1:30].**

Paul certainly knew what it was to suffer for Christ. Suffering for Christ is a token of blessing, not a sign that God has turned His face away.

This concludes chapter 1 in which we have seen the philosophy of Christian living. The chapter is summed up in one verse: "For to me to live Christ, and to die gain."

CHAPTER 2

THEME: Pattern for Christian living—others; mind of Christ—humble; mind of God—exaltation of Christ; mind of Paul—things of Christ; mind of Timothy— like-minded with Paul; mind of Epaphroditus—the work of Christ

In the first chapter we saw the *philosophy* of Christian living summed up in one verse: "For to me to live is Christ, and to die is gain." Christ was the very center of Paul's life. Now in this chapter we come to the *pattern* for Christian living, which is the mind of Christ, as we shall see.

It cannot be by imitation. I hear people talking today about following Jesus. I sometimes would like to ask these folk what they mean by that—especially when their lives do not conform to what they are saying. Are they trying to imitate Jesus? When Paul says here that Christ is the pattern for Christian living, he is not talking about imitation. He is talking about *impartation.* That is, the mind of Christ should be in us, and it can be there only by the power of the Spirit of God.

I learned a long time ago that when Vernon McGee does things, they are not only not done well, they are done wrong—always. I am accused of being rather strong-willed, and I have a tendency to move ahead on my own volition. But when I do that, I stub my toe. Then I say, "Lord, I'm ready now for You to take over." It has been wonderful to see how the Lord does take over.

We need to learn to sit back and watch the Spirit of God move. That doesn't mean that we simply sit and twiddle our thumbs. Of course we carry on the program that God has given us to carry on, but the power and the dynamic come from the Spirit of God.

In this chapter is one of the greatest theological statements made in Scripture concerning the person of Christ. Down through the centuries one of the most controversial issues has come out of that theological statement. In fact, it is the thing that probably divided Europe—it had more to do with it than anything else. The theory promoted was the kenosis theory, which is that at Christ's incarnation He emptied Himself of His deity. This chapter will make it clear that He did not empty Himself of His deity.

THE PATTERN FOR CHRISTIAN LIVING—OTHERS

Before we get into the controversial issue, let's notice the practical side—this is a practical epistle.

If there be therefore any consolation in Christ, if any comfort of love, if any fellowship of the Spirit, if any bowels and mercies [Phil. 2:1].

The "if" which begins this verse is not the *if* of condition—this is not a conditional clause. You will find that many times Paul uses *if* as an argument rather than a condition. Paul is a logical thinker. It has been said that if you do not find Paul logical, you are not reading him aright. It would be more accurate to translate it: "*Since* there is consolation in Christ, and *since* there is comfort of love, and *since* there is the fellowship of the Spirit, and *since* there are bowels [tenderness] and mercy."

Now in view of all this, Paul says:

Fulfil ye my joy, that ye be like-minded, having the same love, being of one accord, of one mind [Phil. 2:2].

Even though he is in prison, he is rejoicing in the Lord, but he says that he would rejoice even more if he knew the gospel was working in the lives of the Philippian believers.

"That ye be like-minded, having the same love, being of one accord, of one mind." You see, there had been a little difficulty, as we noted before, in the Philippian church—not much, but a little. Paul wants them to be of one mind.

He is not asking them to be carbon copies of each other. In most churches there are two groups of people: one group *for* the pastor and one group *against* the pastor. The folk that comprise these groups are not thinking for themselves but are carbon copies of the group leaders.

To be of one mind is to let the mind of Christ be in you. That permits differences of expressions, differences in gifts, differences in methods of service, even differences in minor doctrines. We won't be beating each other on the head because we disagree on these things. If we have the mind of Christ, we will agree on the major tenets of the faith.

Let nothing be done through strife or vainglory; but in lowliness of mind let each esteem other better than themselves [Phil. 2:3].

You remember that Paul has mentioned this before. He said that there were some people who were preaching Christ out of envy and strife. Now he says, "Let nothing be done through strife or vainglory." I would say most of the difficulties in the church today are not due to doctrinal differences. They are due to strife and envy. Some people just naturally cause trouble. If we could follow this injunction, "Let nothing be done through strife or vainglory," I think it would solve 90 percent or maybe even 100 percent of the problems in churches today.

If you are doing something through strife in the church, you had better not do it at all. The same is true if you do things because you expect to be recognized. One of the reasons I don't like to go to organizational meetings is that I get tired of people having to thank Mrs. So-and-so because she brought a bouquet of petunias or Mr. So-and-so because he brought in an extra chair—and you don't dare leave out anyone because if you do, you will be in trouble. Do Christians need to be recognized and complimented and commended for things they do? "Let nothing be done through strife or vainglory"—trying to make a name for yourself.

"But in lowliness of mind let each esteem other better than themselves." Perhaps this was the problem between Euodias and Syntyche. It may be that each felt she was being put down by the other.

If this verse were obeyed, I believe it would solve the problems in most of the music departments in our churches. It would eliminate this attitude: "Why don't they call on me to sing? I have a much better voice than So-and-so." The same could be said for problems on boards and on committees. It would eliminate the "power struggle" that goes on in some churches among the church officers.

> **Look not every man on his own things, but every man also on the things of others [Phil. 2:4].**

Others! That is an important word.

I was absolutely overwhelmed to get a letter from another broadcaster with a gift for our broadcast enclosed. It came from a man whose broadcast is carried on one of the same stations as our broadcast in the state of Florida. He wrote, "What a blessing your broadcast is." I don't know anything about this man's broadcast, but I can tell you something about his person. He was exhibiting the mind of Christ. He was carrying out the admonition of this verse: "Look not every man on his own things, but every man also on the things of others." His letter was a very humbling experience for me.

"Others" is the key to this passage. It is the Christian faith which first made that word *others* important. Why did Christ come from heaven's glory to this earth? It was for others. Why should we carry the gospel? For others. To think of others rather than ourselves is having the mind of Christ.

MIND OF CHRIST—HUMBLE

Now Paul is going to tell us about the mind of Christ.

> **Let this mind be in you, which was also in Christ Jesus [Phil. 2:5].**

The mind of Christ—what is the one thing that characterized it? Humility. You may recall that in Ephesians 4 we are told, ". . . walk worthy of the vocation wherewith ye are called." Then it goes on to describe this: "With all lowliness and meekness, with longsuffering, forbearing one another in love" (Eph. 4:1–2). That is the mind of Christ.

You and I can't be humble. We can't be meek. We are not made that way. We want to stand on our own two feet and have our little say. All of us are like that. Don't say you are not, because you really are. None of us wants to be offended. None of us wants to be ignored. We develop hang-ups if we are brought up in such a way that we have been trampled on.

I heard about the son of a very fine minister who had become a vagrant. Why? It was because he had an older brother who was a brilliant fellow. This boy was always hearing about the brilliant things his older brother was doing. So he just went in the opposite direction, rebelling against it. That is the natural reaction of the natural man. It wouldn't even help matters to go to the boy and say, "Now listen, son, you just ignore all that." He is not going to ignore it. A man who is not born again is not even in the territory of being willing to take a humble place.

We come now to one of the great theological statements in the Scripture. Some consider it the greatest doctrinal statement in the New Testament relative to the person of Christ, and it is know as the *kenosis*, the "emptying." This passage will make it clear that He did not empty Himself of His deity. It will give us the seven steps of humiliation which Christ took. I wish I were capable of sketching for you the magnitude of what is being said in these next few verses. I wish we could grasp how high He was and how low He came. The billions of light years across known space are nothing compared to the distance He came.

We find here seven steps downward. Then we have listed for us seven steps upward, the exaltation of Christ. First, then, in humiliation, we see the mind of Christ. Then we will see the mind of God. It is in the mind of God the Father to exalt the Lord Jesus Christ. If you want to know what you can do that will put you in the will of God—I don't know where you are to go or what you *do*—but I can tell you this: Since it is the purpose of God the Father to exalt Jesus Christ, I believe that is the will of God for every one of us. We are to exalt Jesus Christ, wherever we are and in whatever we do. We are to be one with the Father in this ultimate purpose of the exalation of Jesus Christ.

The *first* step downward was when He left heaven's glory. He came down and down and down to this earth, all the way to where we are. You and I cannot even conceive of what a big step it was from heaven's glory all the way down to this earth. Absolutely, it is beyond human comprehension to understand what our Lord really did for us.

Who, being in the form of God, thought it not robbery to be equal with God [Phil. 2:6].

This is, I confess, a rather stilted translation. When Christ was at the right hand of God the Father, He wasn't hanging on to His position. There was no danger of His losing His place in the Godhead because of any lack on His part or because of the ability and ambition of a contender. He hadn't gone to school to learn to become God; He had not advanced from another position. He *was* God. It wasn't as if the Lord Jesus had to say to God the Father, "Now You be sure to keep My position for Me while I'm gone for thirty-three years. Keep a sharp eye out for Gabriel—I think he would like to have My place." I am not being irreverent; I am trying to show you that this was not something that He had to hold on to. The position belonged to Him. He was God.

Nor did He leave heaven reluctantly. At no time did He say, "Oh, I just hate to leave heaven. I don't want to go down on that trip." He came joyfully. ". . . for the *joy* that was set before him . . ." (Heb. 12:2, italics mine) He endured the cross. He said, ". . . Lo, I come (in the volume of the book it is written of me,) to do thy will, O God" (Heb. 10:7). He came to this earth with joy. He was not releasing something that He wanted to hold on to when He came to this earth.

Now we see the *second* step down.

But made himself of no reputation, and took upon him the form of a servant, and was made in the likeness of men [Phil. 2:7].

"Made himself of no reputation" means *to empty*—the Greek word is kenoō. The kenosis theory derives its name from the word kenoō. Christ emptied Himself. The question is: Of what did He empty Himself? There are those who say He emptied Himself of His deity. All of the Gnostics in the early church propounded the first heresy that He emptied Himself of His deity, that the deity entered into Him at the time of His baptism and left Him at the cross. Well, this theory is not substantiated anywhere in the Word of God. He emptied Himself of something, but it was not of His deity. He was 100 percent God when He was a baby reclining helplessly on the bosom of Mary. Even at that time He could have spoken this universe out of existence because He was God. There was never a moment when He was not God. The apostle John writes, "In the beginning was the Word, and the Word was with God, and the Word was God. The same was in the beginning with God. All things were made by him; and without him was not any thing made that was made. . . . And the Word was made flesh, and dwelt among us . . ." (John 1:1–3, 14).

Well, then, of what did the Lord Jesus empty Himself when He came to this earth? I believe that He emptied Himself of the *prerogatives* of deity. He lived on this earth with certain limitations, but they were self-limitations. There was never a moment when He wasn't God. And He was not less God because He was man, yet He emptied Himself of His prerogatives of deity.

The few shepherds and wise men, and even the multitude of angels, were a sorry turnout for the Son of God when He came to this earth. Not only should that crowd have been there, but the whole universe should have been there. All of God's created intelligences should have been there. The hierarchy of Rome should have been there. There should not have been just a few wise men from the East. They should have come from the West, and the North, and the South. And the temple in Jerusalem should have been empty that day—they should all have gone down to Bethlehem. But they didn't.

Why didn't He force them to come? Because He had laid aside His prerogatives of deity. He was willing to be born in a dirty, filthy place—not the pretty, clean stable of Christmas pageants and Christmas cards. He was willing to grow to manhood in a miserable town named Nazareth. He was willing to be an unknown carpenter. He could have had the *shekinah* glory with Him all the time, but He didn't. He didn't have a halo around His head as we see in so many paintings of Him. Judas had to kiss Him the night He was betrayed so that the crowd would know which was the man they were to capture.

He didn't stand out from other men by some kind of inner light or glory around Him. He was a human being, but He was God manifest in the flesh. He laid aside the prerogatives of His deity.

Can we be sure of that? I think we can. After He had finished His ministry, He gathered His own about Him on His last night on earth, and He prayed a very wonderful prayer to His heavenly Father. One thing He said in that prayer was this: "And now, O Father, glorify thou me with thine own self with the glory which I had with thee before the world was" (John 17:5). Notice this carefully: He prayed to have His glory restored. He did not pray to have His deity restored, because He had never given up His deity. But now that He is returning to heaven, He is asking that His glory, the glory light, a prerogative of deity, be restored. Obviously He had laid that aside. "Who, being in the form of God, thought it not robbery to be equal with God: But made himself of no reputation."

The third step downward in the humiliation of Christ is this: "And took upon him the form of a servant."

Jesus came to this earth as a servant. He worked as a carpenter. I suppose if you had lived in Nazareth in that day, you could have gone by the shop where Jesus worked and told Him you needed some repair work done at your house—"I have a door that is coming off the hinges; I wonder if You would come and fix it?" I think He would have said, "I'll be right over." You see, He took upon Himself the form of a servant. He could have been born in Caesar's palace. He was a king, but He never made that claim during those early years—in fact, He didn't make it until He rode into Jerusalem in the so-called Triumphal Entry.

He came into this world as a working man, a humble man, a little man. Not only did He humiliate Himself to become a human being, but He came among the majority where most of us are today. He was one of the little people.

The prophet Isaiah wrote that Christ would come as a "root of Jesse" (see Isa. 11:10). As a young preacher I often wondered why Isaiah didn't call Him a root out of David. Well, I have discovered the reason. When Jesus was born, Mary, who was in the line of David (and Joseph, who was also in the Davidic line by another route), was a peasant. They were working folk living in that little, miserable, gentile town called Nazareth. Then wasn't Jesus in the line of David? Oh, yes. David was anointed king, but his father Jesse was a farmer in Bethlehem, and his line had dropped back to the place of a peasant. Our Lord was born into a peasant family.

"He took upon him the form of a servant."

The *fourth* step in His humiliation is this: "And was made in the likeness of men."

For years this did not impress me at all, because I am a man and I like being a man. I couldn't see that being a man was a humiliation. I think there is a dignity about being a human being that is quite wonderful. How can it be humbling?

Let me give you a very homely illustration that I trust might be as helpful to you as it is to me. I confess it is rather ridiculous, but it will illustrate the humiliation of Christ in His incarnation.

When we first came to California in 1940, we had the experience of living in a place where the bugs and the ants are not killed off in the wintertime. We got here the first of November and had not been here long until I found in the kitchen one morning a freeway of ants coming into the sink. They were coming down one side and going back on the other side. Also I found they had discovered the sugar bowl, and they had a freeway in and out of it. I don't know about you, but I don't want ants in the sink and I don't want ants in the sugar bowl. So I began to investigate and learned that the thing we had to do was to kill them. Now I'm just not sadistic; I'm not brutal; I don't like to kill things. But I began to kill ants. I got ant poison, and we got rid of the ants. Then when we moved over to our own home, here were ants. They had found out where we'd moved. I have a wonderful Christian friend who is in the bug-killing business. He comes to my place twice a year, sprays everything—under the house, under the eaves, the trees—everything, and you can't find an ant on my place.

Now I do not know this to be a fact, but I have a notion that the ants had a protest meeting around my lot. Maybe they carried banners that read, "Down with McGee. He hates ants!" But, frankly, I don't hate ants. That's not my hang-up at all. If I had some way of communicating with those ants and getting a message to them, I'd say, "Look here. I don't hate you. Just stay out of the sugar bowl, and stay out of the sink. I'll put sugar and water outside for you—I'd be glad to do that if you'd just stay outside." But I do not know how to get that message over to the ants—except by becoming an ant. Now suppose that I had the power to become an ant. (If I *could* do it, I would *not* do it because I know some folk who would step on me if I were an ant!) But listen, if I could become an ant—from where I am now down to the position of an ant—that would be humiliation, wouldn't it? I'd *hate* to become an ant. But, my friend, that is nothing compared to what my Lord did when He left heaven's glory and became a man, when He took upon Himself our humanity, when He was made in the likeness of men.

And being found in fashion as a man, he humbled himself, and became obedient unto death, even the death of the cross [Phil. 2:8].

The *fifth* step in our Lord's humiliation is that He humbled Himself. "And being found in fashion as a man, he humbled himself." You and I have been humbled by someone doing or saying something which has been humiliating to us. But notice that Christ "humbled himself." This is a most difficult thing to do.

One of the finest things I ever heard about John Wesley was concerning an incident when he was about to cross a brook over which was a very narrow bridge, just wide enough for one person. As he was starting over, he met a liberal preacher of that day. This preacher swelled up and said, "I never give way to a fool." John Wesley looked at him for a moment, smiled, and began to back off, saying, "I always do." My friend, it is difficult to take that humble place, but it has made me think a great deal more of John Wesley. We find it difficult to humble ourselves, but our Lord humbled Himself.

Many of us have had humbling experiences. I am reminded of a summer conference at which I was speaking years ago. One of the speakers at this conference was a most dignified Englishman. He was a gifted speaker and very dignified. He was shocked when I wore a sport shirt even on the platform. To him that was the unpardonable sin. He wore a white shirt, collar, and tie; in fact, he wore a frock coat for the evening services! Well, one afternoon it rained, and in the auditorium a window glass had been broken out so that it had rained in on the platform. In those early days all the speakers in any week would march onto the platform every night, regardless of who was bringing the message. On that particular night I walked behind this dignified, formally dressed Englishman, and when he hit that wet spot on the platform, his feet went out from under him. Oh, how he sprawled! And, you know, everybody laughed. I laughed so hard I had to leave the platform. After I went back and sat down on the platform, I thought I never could quit laughing. The next night we started in as usual, and he was right ahead of me again. I reached over and said, "Say, it'd be nice to have a repeat performance tonight." "Oh," he said, "wasn't that humbling!" Yes, he was humbled, but he did not humble himself. Many times we are humbled, are we not? But we do not humble ourselves.

The Lord Jesus humbled Himself, and that is altogether different.

We come now to the *sixth* step in His humiliation: "and [He] became obedient unto death." Death is a very humiliating sort of thing. It is not natural. Sometimes at funerals I hear people say, "Doesn't he look natural?" It is generally said by some well-meaning friend who wants to comfort the loved ones. I don't know why it would be a source of comfort to think that Grandpa looks natural in death. I bite my lip to keep from saying, "No, he doesn't look natural." Death is not natural. God didn't create man to die. Man dies because of sin, because of his transgression. Death came by the transgression of one man, and that man was Adam, and death has passed down to all men. Death is not natural. God did not create man to die.

Now when the Lord Jesus came to this earth, He was a little different from the rest of us. You and I came to live. I honestly don't want to die; I want to live. I have come to the most fruitful part of my ministry, and I want to live as long as the Lord will let me. But the Lord Jesus was born to die. He came to this earth to die. He didn't have to die, but He "became obedient unto death" and gave Himself up willingly. I have to die, but I don't want to. He didn't have to die, but He wanted to. Why? In order that He might save you and me if we will put our trust in Him. This is what He said: "As the Father knoweth me, even so know I the Father: and I lay down my life for the sheep. . . . Therefore doth my Father love me, because I lay down my life, that I might take it again. No man taketh it from me, but I lay it down of myself. I have power to lay it down, and I have power to take it again . . ." (John 10:15, 17–18).

The *seventh* and last step in the humiliation of Christ is "even the death of the cross." Not only did He become obedient unto death, but to the death of the *cross.* This would make a greater impact on our consciousness if we said that Christ died in the electric chair or the gas chamber or by the hangman's noose. It was that kind of disgraceful death. He came from the highest glory to the lowest place of humiliation. Why did He do it? Let's go back to the word *others.* "Look not every man on his own things, but every man also on the things of others." He left all the glory of heaven and came down to this earth, became a man, and suffered the death of a criminal for others—for you and me. Thank God for that! This is the mind of Christ.

MIND OF GOD—EXALTATION OF CHRIST

Now the mind of God the Father is to glorify Christ. We have seen the seven steps downward; now we will see the seven steps upward. The mind of God is the exaltation of Christ.

> **Wherefore God also hath highly exalted him, and given him a name which is above every name [Phil. 2:9].**

Here is the *first* step up: "God also hath highly exalted him." The supreme purpose of God the Father in this universe today is that Jesus Christ be glorified in the universe which He created and that He be glorified on the earth where man dwells, where man rebelled against God.

The thing that makes this little earth significant and important is the death of Christ down here—nothing else. Astronomers tell us that we are a little speck in space, and if our little world were to be blotted out, it wouldn't make any difference to the universe. And that is absolutely true. Someone else has said that man is a "disease on the epidermis of a minor planet." That is what we are! The thing that has lent dignity to man and has caused him to look up into the heavens and sing the doxology is the fact that Jesus Christ came to this earth and died on the cross for him. "Wherefore God also hath highly exalted him."

Now the second step: "and given him a name which is above every name." The next time you take His name in vain, think of this. God intends to exalt that name that you use as a curse word and drag in the mud. The other day a pilot who stepped off a plane on which a bomb had exploded—and it was almost a miracle that he was able to land the plane—just stood over at the side of the crowd and said, "Jesus Christ, Jesus Christ!" I don't know if he was saying it as profanity—God have mercy on him if he did it that way. I hope that it was a prayer. The name of Jesus Christ will be exalted above the names of all the great men of this world and above the names of all the angels in glory.

That at the name of Jesus every knee should bow, of things in heaven, and things in earth, and things under the earth [Phil. 2:10].

In this verse we find the next three steps of Christ's exaltation.

The third step: "That at the name of Jesus"—*Jesus* means "Savior." Before His birth in Bethlehem, the angel said, ". . . thou shalt call his name JESUS: for he shall save his people from their sins" (Matt. 1:21). Now notice the reference to prophecy: "Now all this was done, that it might be fulfilled which was spoken of the Lord by the prophet, saying, Behold, a virgin shall be with child, and shall bring forth a son, and they shall call his name Emmanuel, which being interpreted is, God with us" (Matt. 1:22–23).

Can you show me any place in the Bible where He was called Emmanuel? When I entered the ministry, I had no problem with "Behold a virgin shall conceive." Since He is God, how else could He get into the human family except by a miraculous birth? But the thing that did cause a problem in this verse was, "He shall be called Emmanuel" because I couldn't find any place where they called Him Emmanuel. "Well, then," you may say, "that prophecy was not fulfilled."

Oh, my friend, this is one of the most wonderful fulfillments of prophecy you can imagine. The angel said, "Call Him Jesus because

He'll save His people from their sins." Now think through this. You couldn't call me *Jesus*—I can't even save myself. Neither would it be accurate to call you *Jesus* because you can't save yourself. You see, all of us are in the same ship today. The human family is on a sinking ship, and it's going down. If there is to be a Savior, He's got to come from the outside. There are those who want to throw out a lifeline. But to do that is like being on a ship that is sinking, and somebody on the top deck says to those down in the steerage, "Let me throw you a lifeline." But the top deck is going down too! You see, the rope has to come from some place other than the human ship. No human being can be a Savior. "You shall call His name *Jesus* because He is going to save His people from their sins." How can He save His people from their sins? Because He will be Emmanuel, God with us. That little Baby who came yonder to Bethlehem is God with us. He took upon Himself, not the likeness of angels, but our humanity. He is Emmanuel, God with us. And because He is that, He can be called Jesus. And friend, nobody else can properly be called *Jesus*.

Now God says, "I'm going to exalt the name which was given to Him when He came to earth above every other name."

Now notice the *fourth* step of His exaltation: "Of things in heaven."

And the *fifth* step: "And things in earth."

And the *sixth* step: "And things under the earth." This verse is used by the Restitutionalists to support their theory that ultimately everybody will be saved. We had a spokesman for this cult in Los Angeles for many years. He made the statement that Judas Isacriot and the Devil would be walking down the streets of heaven together because ultimately all would be saved. Of course it was unfortunate that he used this verse because when you compare it with Colossians 1:20, you see its true meaning. The subject in the Philippians passage is the lordship of Jesus. God has highly exalted Him, that at the name of Jesus every knee must bow, in heaven, in earth, and under the earth. That is, even hell will have to bow to Him because He is the Lord. He is God. But merely bowing does not imply salvation. Colossians 1:20 is not talking about lordship, but about Christ's reconciling work, His redemptive work. And what was reconciled? What was redeemed? Was hell included? No. The things *under the earth* are not mentioned here. Why? Because this verse is talking about redemption, and there is no redemption in hell. By putting these two verses together it is clear that those in hell who bow to Jesus are merely acknowledging His lordship. "That at the name of Jesus every knee should bow, of things in heaven, and things in earth, and things under the earth." Here now is the *seventh* and final step of Christ's exaltation:

And that every tongue should confess that Jesus Christ is Lord, to the glory of God the Father [Phil. 2:11].

Every tongue shall "confess that Jesus Christ is Lord." That doesn't mean that every tongue will confess Him as Savior. It is interesting that even in hell they must recognize the lordship of Jesus, which will, I think, increase their anguish.

I want to give a word of caution here. Be very careful about calling Jesus your Lord if He is not your Lord. He made the statement that many would call Him Lord, Lord, and even perform miracles in His name, yet He will say, "I never knew you" (see Matt. 7:21–23). My friend, you had better know Him as your Savior before you say He is your Lord. If He is your Savior, then you can become obedient to Him as your Lord.

I don't even like to hear people sing, "What a Friend we have in Jesus." We have a friend in Him all right, but listen to the words of Jesus: "Ye are my friends, *if* ye do whatsoever I command you" (John 15:14, italics mine). We can call Him our friend if we do what He commands us to do. He is not our Lord unless we obey Him.

MIND OF PAUL—THINGS OF CHRIST

We have been learning about the mind of Christ. We have seen it is not something which can be imitated. "Let this mind be in you which was also in Christ Jesus" can only happen by *impartation*. It is the work of the Spirit of God within us which will produce the fruit of meekness or humility in our lives.

Now we are going to see the mind of Christ as it walked down the Roman roads. We will see it lived in Roman homes and in a Roman jail. We will see three examples given to us: the mind of Paul, the mind of Timothy, and the mind of Epaphroditus (pastor of the church at Philippi). In this heathen empire there were these three men who exhibited the mind of Christ and there may have been three million more, but these are the ones who are presented to us in this epistle.

> **Wherefore, my beloved, as ye have always obeyed, not as in my presence only, but now much more in my absence, work out your own salvation with fear and trembling [Phil. 2:12].**

"Salvation" in this verse is used, I believe, in a general sense. Paul is talking about working out their problems which they had in the church and working out the problems in their own Christian lives. He is not there to help them and is not sure that he ever will be there again because he is in a Roman prison. So he tells them to work out their "own salvation with fear and trembling."

A preacher was reading this verse of Scripture in the morning service. A little girl whispered to her mother, "Mother, you can't work *out* salvation unless it has first been worked *in*, can you?" Now that is a very good question. The next verse answers it.

> **For it is God which worketh in you both to will and to do of his good pleasure [Phil. 2:13].**

So God works out that which He had worked in. If God has saved you, He has saved you by faith—plus nothing. God is not accepting any kind of good works for salvation. But *after* you are saved, God talks to you about your works. The salvation that He worked in by faith is a salvation He will work out also.

Calvin expressed it this way: "Faith alone saves, but the faith that saves is not alone." James states it like this: "Even so faith, if it hath not works, is dead, being alone. Yea, a man may say, Thou hast faith, and I have works: shew me thy faith without thy works, and I will shew thee my faith by my works" (James 2:17–18). Only God can see the heart; He knows our true condition. He knows if I have saving faith; He knows if you have saving faith. But your neighbor can't see your faith. The only thing he can see is the works of faith. True faith will work itself out so that the people around us will be able to tell that we are different, that we are Christians. We don't need to wear a placard or some sort of symbol to identify ourselves as Christians.

Paul will talk about that faith which will work itself out in the lives of the Philippian believers.

Do all things without murmurings and disputings [Phil. 2:14].

Don't accept an office in the church or in the Sunday school if you have to grumble about doing it. That absolutely wrecks more Christian work than anything else. Do *all* things without grumbling or disputing.

That ye may be blameless and harmless, the sons of God, without rebuke, in the midst of a crooked and perverse nation, among whom ye shine as lights in the world [Phil. 2:15].

Be like a light. When we go out at night we see the stars up there. When God looks down on this dark world, He sees those who are His own as little lights down here. The children sing "This Little Light of Mine." Well, my friend, that's exactly what it is. Paul says, "Among whom ye shine as lights in the world." As the stars are up there, we are down here.

Holding forth the word of life; that I may rejoice in the day of Christ, that I have not run in vain, neither laboured in vain [Phil. 2:16].

Life and light are related. When we hold forth the Word of Life, we are lights in the world. Paul rejoices when he hears that the Philippian believers are manifesting their faith in good works. These believers were very close to the heart of Paul because they were his converts.

Yea, and if I be offered upon the sacrifice and service of your faith, I joy, and rejoice with you all [Phil. 2:17].

Here is one of the most wonderful verses in the entire Word of God. It pictures what the Christian life really should be. He is referring to one of the earliest offerings in the Old Testament. When we go back to Genesis 35:14, we find that Jacob set up a pillar at Bethel, "and he poured a drink offering thereon, and he poured oil thereon." Then in the books of Leviticus and Numbers the sacrifices are described. We learned that there was a drink offering which was to be added to the burnt offering and the meal offering. It was never added to the sin offering or the trespass offering. It was a most unusual offering in that it had nothing to do with redemption; it had nothing to do with the person of Christ. They would bring in a skin of wine and just pour it on the sacrifice which was being consumed by fire. What happened to it? It would go up in steam and disappear.

Paul is saying, "I want my life to be poured out like a drink offering on the offering of Christ." Paul knows that the Lord Jesus Christ made the supreme sacrifice. He wanted his life to be a drink offering—just poured out to go up in steam. He wanted to be so consumed and obscured that all that is seen is just Jesus Christ. He wanted Christ to receive all the honor and the glory. This was the mind of Paul. I can think of no higher wish for the Christian life.

For the same cause also do ye joy, and rejoice with me [Phil. 2:18].

In other words, "If your life commends the gospel, my life is just poured out as a drink offering. Together we'll rejoice over this." It is a walk in humility. Only a person with the mind of Christ could be so poured out as a drink offering. How gloriously wonderful that is.

Paul ends on a note of joy and rejoicing. Today we often rejoice over the wrong things. We need to rejoice over the fact that Jesus died for us and that we can serve Him. When we hear of someone whom God is using or hear of a wonderful church where people are being saved and built up in the faith, we ought to rejoice. If we are walking in humility, we will rejoice at the success of others. We have too much strife and vainglory. That was hurting the cause of Christ in Paul's day, and it still hurts the cause of Christ. The mind of Christ in the believer will bring joy and will bring glory to God.

MIND OF TIMOTHY—LIKE-MINDED WITH PAUL

But I trust in the Lord Jesus to send Timotheus shortly unto you, that I also may be of good comfort, when I know your state [Phil. 2:19].

Timothy was Paul's spiritual son. Paul had great confidence in him. He could trust Timothy to care for the state of the Philippian believers.

For I have no man likeminded, who will naturally care for your state [Phil. 2:20].

Here we have described the mind of Timothy, and we find that he is like-minded with Paul. Since he was like-minded with Paul, it means that he had the mind of Christ, and he was characterized by humility. We don't need a National Council or World Council of Churches to bring men together. In fact, we don't need any organization to bring them together. If they both have the mind of Christ, they are together.

Timothy had been faithful to Paul. Sometimes a convert later turns against the person who led him to the Lord. This is like a child turning against a parent. Paul had had that happen to him, but Timothy was faithful to him. Paul was sending him to the Philippian believers because he could trust him. It is wonderful to have men like-minded with Christ so they can work together.

For all seek their own, not the things which are Jesus Christ's [Phil. 2:21].

There were many others who were seeking their own glory. They wanted to make a name for themselves. Because they were seeking their own glory, they were willing to belittle Paul.

How do you respect others who are standing for the Word of God today? When I hear a man of God being criticized, I recognize that somewhere there is strife and vainglory. The mind of Christ will not allow you to criticize another man who stands for Christ. Paul says, "I can't trust these other men."

> **But ye know the proof of him, that, as a son with the father, he hath served with me in the gospel [Phil. 2:22].**

People speak a lot about togetherness in our day. There can be no more togetherness than for two people to have the mind of Christ. They are together even though they may be miles apart. That is why there is such a bond between fellow Christians who have the mind of Christ.

When a Christian young man and a Christian young lady fall in love, there is a togetherness that you cannot have in just a sexual marriage. A relationship that is simply physical can be bought on any street corner. But when a husband and wife have the mind of Christ, they are really together. There is no human ceremony that can bring two people together in that way. It is a glorious, wonderful relationship.

> **Him therefore I hope to send presently, so soon as I shall see how it will go with me.**
>
> **But I trust in the Lord that I also myself shall come shortly [Phil. 2:23-24].**

Paul wanted Timothy to be the one who would bring them the message about what was going to happen to him there in the prison. Paul had hopes that he would be released from prison. Tradition says that he was released from prison and had quite an itinerant ministry after this, although this is not recorded in Scripture. When the Christians were persecuted under Nero, naturally Paul, the leader, was brought back and executed.

MIND OF EPHAPHRODITUS—THE
WORK OF CHRIST

Epaphroditus was another who had the mind of Christ. He and Paul and Timothy were together, brethren in the Lord, serving the Lord. Remember that he is the pastor of the church in Philippi.

> **Yet I supposed it necessary to send to you Epaphroditus, my brother, and companion in labour, and fellowsoldier, but your messenger, and he that ministered to my wants [Phil. 2:25].**

Paul had founded the church at Philippi, but Epaphroditus was not jealous of Paul. Paul loved Epaphroditus because he had the mind of Christ and Paul could trust him. He calls him "my brother, and my companion in labour, and my fellowsoldier." Paul says, "He is my fellowsoldier—he fights with me. He doesn't stick a knife in my back when I'm away. He doesn't side with my enemies. He stands shoulder to shoulder with me for the faith."

"But your messenger, and he that ministered to my wants." He was of practical help to Paul who is confined there in chains.

> **For he longed after you all, and was full of heaviness, because that ye had heard that he had been sick [Phil. 2:26].**

This is almost humorous here. Epaphroditus got sick, and word was sent back to the church at Philippi that their own pastor was sick. He longed for them—he probably was a little homesick also. Then when he heard that the church back there was mourning for him because he was sick, he had a relapse because it hurt him that they were hurt because he was sick! There was sort of a vicious circle set in motion here. But it was good because it revealed the marvelous relationship between the church at Philippi and their pastor.

In my conference ministry I speak in many churches, and I have

that I can judge a church by its attitude toward a pastor who
s and teaches the Word of God. When a deacon takes me aside
s, "Dr. McGee, we have a fine young pastor, and he is preaching the Word of God," this rejoices my heart. But sometimes a deacon
takes me aside and says, "Say, how do we get rid of a pastor like we
have? He is too opinionated, too dogmatic, and he wants to run
things." I ask him, "Is he teaching and preaching the Word?" When
the deacon's answer is, "Oh, yes, but we have had that all along," I can
see that the Word has had no effect upon that man. If his feeling is
shared by the church in general, that church is doomed. The rejection
of a Bible-teaching preacher is the death knell of many churches
across this land of ours. You see, the Devil has been very clever. He has
shifted his attack from the Word of God itself to the man who teaches
the Word of God. I find this is true across the length and breadth of our
nation. The real test of a church is its attitude toward its pastor.

Epaphroditus was greatly loved by his church, and that speaks
well for the church in Philippi.

**For indeed he was sick nigh unto death: but God had
mercy on him; and not on him only, but on me also, lest I
should have sorrow upon sorrow [Phil. 2:27].**

Let me point out something here that you may not notice. Many sincere believers today hold the theory that Christians should not be sick,
that they should trust God to heal them. Let me ask a question: Why
didn't Paul heal Epaphroditus? He was so sick he almost died! You
see, Paul and the other apostles had "sign gifts" because they did not
have what we have today, a New Testament. When Paul started out
with the gospel message, nothing of the New Testament had been
written. Paul himself wrote 1 Thessalonians, the second book of the
New Testament to be penned. When he went into a new territory with
his message, what was his authority? He had no authority, except sign
gifts, which included the gift of healing. But now Paul is nearing the
conclusion of his ministry. You will remember that Paul had a thorn in
the flesh which the Lord Jesus would not remove. Instead, He gave

Paul the grace to bear it. Then you remember that Timothy had stomach trouble. If Paul had been a faith healer, why hadn't he healed Timothy? Actually, he told him to take a little wine for his stomach's sake. And in 2 Timothy 4:20 he said that he had left Trophimus in Miletum sick. Why hadn't he healed him? And now Paul says he has this young preacher, Epaphroditus, with him, and he was so sick he almost died. Paul didn't heal him. Rather, he gives all the credit to God; he says that God had mercy on him. His healing came about in a natural sort of way. Paul made it a matter of prayer, and God heard and answered prayer. Why hadn't Paul used his gift of healing? Because at this late stage, even before the apostles disappeared from the scene, the emphasis was moving back to the Great Physician.

You see, this epistle is emphasizing the mind of Christ, a humble mind. If I were a faith healer, I would be in the limelight; I would be somebody very great and very famous. But I'm not. The Lord Jesus is the Great Physician. When it was first discovered that I had cancer, I received a great number of letters advising me to go to this healer and that healer. No, I didn't go to anyone, my friend, except a very fine cancer specialist and the Great Physician. I had an appointment with Him and I told Him I wanted to live. I turned over my case to Him. And He gets the credit for what happened to me.

So here is Paul the apostle toward the end of his ministry putting no emphasis on healing whatsoever. He has a sick preacher with him, but he does not exercise the gift of healing that he had. Why? Because Paul is shifting the emphasis where it should be, upon the person of the Lord Jesus Christ.

Now Paul is sending Epaphroditus back to them.

I sent him therefore the more carefully, that, when ye see him again, ye may rejoice, and that I may be the less sorrowful [Phil. 2:28].

Paul wants them to rejoice, not sorrow. "And that I may be the less sorrowful"—he was disturbed about the church in Philippi because it had been morning instead of rejoicing.

Receive him therefore in the Lord with all gladness; and hold such in reputation [Phil. 2:29].

How gracious Paul was with this preacher from Philippi! A man like Epaphroditus should be respected and loved.

And, my friend, we should respect the one who is teaching the Word of God. If he has a gift of teaching which God is using, both the gift and the individual should be respected. Our attention should be focused upon the Word of God. I just don't participate anymore in conventions and seminars that focus attention on problems—the drug problem, the alcohol problem, the sex problem, the youth problems, and the senior citizen problems—and offer psychological solutions for them. My friend, the problem is that we don't get back to the Word of God. It is the Word of God that reveals Christ and the mind of Christ.

Because for the work of Christ he was nigh unto death, not regarding his life, to supply your lack of service toward me [Phil. 2:30].

Epaphroditus was doing the work of Christ. He had to have the mind of Christ to do that.

It sends chills up and down my spine to read about these men. This is in the first century, at the time of the Roman Empire. The empire of Caesar Augustus moved out and took over the world. The law of Rome became supreme everywhere. There was no mercy shown to anyone, but there was law and order everywhere. There was not a power in that day that could protest against Rome. Then there went out this little man, Paul the apostle, and those who were like-minded with him, and they preached a gospel that there is a God of the universe who, through a redemption that He had wrought on a Roman cross, had provided mercy for mankind. Multitudes turned to the Lord Jesus in that day.

Now I see this little man, Paul the apostle, chained to a Roman soldier. What is he doing? Well, he is witnessing for Christ, and he is rejoicing in the Lord. He has the mind of Christ. Also I see a fine young man, Timothy, walking in that pagan city. You say you cannot live for Christ in a godless society? Look at Timothy. He did pretty well. He had the mind of Christ. And then I take a look at Epaphroditus, a faithful pastor way up yonder in the city of Philippi—it was a Roman colony, but it was a pagan, heathen city. Epaphroditus had the mind of Christ.

Then I look at Vernon McGee, and I say to him, *Stop offering excuses in this day in which you are living!* If these men could have the mind of Christ in the first century, today in the twentieth century right where we are now, you and I can have the mind of Christ. Not by imitation, but by yielding to Him, the Spirit of God can produce in our own lives the mind of Christ. Oh, how desperately this is needed in our day!

CHAPTER 3

THEME: Prize for Christian living; Paul changed his bookkeeping system of the past; Paul changed his purpose for the present; Paul changed his hope for the future

We have seen the *philosophy* of Christian living: "For to me to live is Christ, and to die is gain" (Phil. 1:21). We have seen the *pattern* for Christian living: "Let this mind be in you, which was also in Christ Jesus" (Phil. 2:5). Now we come to the *prize* for Christian living which is summarized in Paul's personal testimony: "I press toward the mark for the prize of the high calling of God in Christ Jesus" (v. 14).

We will see in this chapter that Paul changed his bookkeeping system of the *past*, he changed his purpose for the *present*, and he changed his hope for the *future*. Paul believed that God was going to establish a kingdom on this earth; he never changed his view on that. But he did see that there is a marvelous, wonderful hope for believers in Christ—both Jew and Gentile—the day when Christ will take His own out of the world.

PAUL CHANGED HIS BOOKKEEPING SYSTEM OF THE PAST

Finally, my brethren, rejoice in the Lord. To write the same things to you, to me indeed is not grievous, but for you it is safe [Phil. 3:1].

"Finally, my brethren" gives us the impression that Paul is coming to the conclusion of this epistle. He must have intended this to be a very brief thank-you note to the Philippian believers. But we are just midway in the epistle; so obviously the Spirit of God prompted him to go on.

My wife reminded me in a conference some time ago that when I was speaking I said, "Let me say this to you in the final analysis, and then I'll be through"—then I went on talking another fifteen minutes. She said, "You weren't through at all." So I told her I was just being scriptural, that I was doing it the way Paul did it.

His final message was going to be, "Rejoice in the Lord." I think that would still be his final message if he were here today. He has shown how three men—himself, Timothy, and Epaphroditus—all had the mind of Christ. They were able to rejoice even in sickness and imprisonment. The early church could rejoice amid the fires of persecution.

Besides, Paul is saying that it has been no burden to him to write this letter. He has no burden on his heart such as there had been when he wrote to the Galatians and the Corinthians. The Philippians have been a great joy to him. Now he wants them to rejoice, too. Notice that it is actually a command: "Rejoice in the Lord."

"To write the same things to you, to me indeed is not grievous, but for you it is safe." It is safe for him to write to the Philippians. They were spiritually mature. They loved Paul, and he loved them. He felt close to them. So he says it is not grievous, or irksome, to write to them. It is safe for him to write to them because he knows they will understand.

Beware of dogs, beware of evil workers, beware of the concision [Phil. 3:2].

"Beware of dogs." This is not a word of warning to the mailmen. I once had a dog that hated mailmen, and I don't know why. We changed mailmen several times during the period we had him, and he had the same attitude toward each of them. But Paul is not referring to animals in this verse. We will get some insight into this thinking by turning back to the prophecy of Isaiah, who warned against the false prophets of his day: "His watchmen are blind: they are all ignorant, they are all dumb dogs, they cannot bark; sleeping, lying down, loving to slumber" (Isa. 56:10). Isaiah was warning the people against the false prophets who were attempting to comfort the people and were telling them that everything was fine instead of warning them of coming disaster. The northern kingdom had already gone into captivity because the false prophets had given them a false sense of security. God was warning the southern kingdom not to do the same thing. He was calling the false prophets "dumb dogs." They won't speak out. They won't tell it as it is. Dogs are those who are not declaring the full counsel of God.

We have the same grave danger in our affluent society. Comfort is the word of the day. We look for comfortable places to stay when we are traveling. We enjoy all the creature comforts that we can afford. The desire for comfort has carried over into the church. There is a danger of just comforting the people of the congregation because that is what they would like to have coming from the pulpit.

A prominent member of a congregation which I served left the church because he said I never gave him any comforting messages. I found out later that in his business he was not always ethical. In fact, some considered him very unethical. Frankly, he didn't need messages of comfort. He needed messages of warning. I think that was what he didn't like. It may be that he thought I knew something of his business dealings, which I absolutely did not know at the time. In fact, I have never preached a sermon at any individual in my life. I have tried to preach what the Word of God says. Often that is not a comforting message.

When I went to see my doctor, I tried my best to be evasive with him. I told him that I knew someone who had the same trouble I did and he was given medicine and recovered. As he examined me, he said, "Dr. McGee, if you need medication, I will give it to you, but I don't think you need medication. You are in trouble." Well, that was not a comforting message! He told me candidly, "I'm going to tell you the truth, because if I don't, you will not have confidence in me. You have cancer." I have thanked him for that ever since. I wanted to hear the truth. Don't you want to hear the truth?

In Isaiah's day there were a great many false prophets who were comforting the people when they should have been warning them. Isaiah likens the false prophets to dumb dogs. You see, a good sheep dog is constantly alert to danger. If a lion or a bear makes a foray into the flock, that dog will bark like mad and run it away if he can. He gives warning of the approach of any kind of danger. But the false prophets gave no warning at all. Therefore the southern kingdom had been lulled to sleep and resented Isaiah's effort to arouse them.

America today is in the same position. We are going to sleep, my friend, under the comfortable blanket of affluence. We like the idea of comfort, of getting something for nothing, of taking it easy, of having a good day. My feeling is that somebody ought to do a little barking.

So Paul warned, "Beware of dogs"—beware of men who are constantly comforting you and are not giving you the Word of God.

"Beware of evil workers." This is another group that would actually abuse and use believers. They are not honest.

"Beware of the concision"—he slurred the word *circumcision* and said *concision*. He is saying that they are no longer of the true circumcision, referring to the legalizers, those who were attempting to force Christians to keep the law of Moses for salvation and sanctification.

For we are the circumcision, which worship God in the spirit, and rejoice in Christ Jesus, and have no confidence in the flesh [Phil. 3:3].

"We are the circumcision." What does Paul mean by that? He makes it very clear at the end of the Epistle to the Galatians: "For in Christ Jesus neither circumcision availeth any thing, nor uncircumcision, but a new creature" (Gal. 6:15). The old circumcision is out. God is not looking for a mere external observance. True circumcision is of the heart. It is the new birth, a new heart attitude toward God. True circumcision is being in Christ.

"And have no confidence in the flesh." We do not have confidence in our old nature. We trust Christ alone. We do not look to ourselves for salvation, nor can we live the Christian life in our old nature. It must be Christ in us.

These legalizers would follow Paul in his missionary journeys. After he was gone, they would meet with the believers and say something like this: "Well, we know that brother Paul says we are to have no confidence in the flesh, that we are not to trust the rituals nor the sacrifices, and that the Law won't save us. He does well to say that, because he doesn't have very much to rest upon. He doesn't have the background in Judaism that we do. He says that because of his ignorance and the failure of his life to measure up to the requirements of the Law. So of course he has no confidence in the flesh."

Now Paul is going to answer that.

> **Though I might also have confidence in the flesh. If any other man thinketh that he hath whereof he might trust in the flesh, I more [Phil. 3:4].**

Paul says, "If there is any person who could have confidence in the flesh, then I could have even more confidence." He is willing to stack his religious life against that of any man, and he knows that he could measure up to him and surpass him—"I more."

Now he is going to list seven things in which he trusted at one time. This is religion. If anyone could have been saved by religion, Saul of Tarsus would have been the man.

> **Circumcised the eighth day, of the stock of Israel, of the tribe of Benjamin, an Hebrew of the Hebrews; as touching the law, a Pharisee;**

> **Concerning zeal, persecuting the church; touching the righteousness which is in the law, blameless [Phil. 3:5–6].**

These are still things that people boast about today, but none of them can save you.

1. "Circumcised in the eighth day." This is a basic rite of the Mosaic system. Well, of course he didn't get up out of the crib on the eighth day and go down to the temple or synagogue to have the circumcision performed. It means that his parents took him on his eighth day to be circumcised. He is making it clear that he had godly parents. They reared him according to the Mosaic Law. You will remember that the Lord Jesus also had godly parents who brought Him to the temple to be circumcised.

One of the things that hurt me and held me back in my early ministry was the fact that I had not been brought up in a Christian home. My dad was a heavy drinker who would not darken the door of a church. He was very bitter and very prejudiced. He did make me go to Sunday school, and I thank God for that. But I never saw a Bible or heard a prayer in my home. When I went away to seminary, I did not know even the books of the Bible. I would meet other fellows who had been brought up in Christian homes. They seemed to know so much. I always felt deprived, felt that I had missed something. Well, Paul did not have this handicap. He could say, "I was circumcised on the eighth day," which means he had godly parents.

2. "Of the stock of Israel." Probably many of the Judaizers were half-breeds; Paul was not. He was of the stock of Israel. I think you could have checked Paul's genealogy in the temple in that day. Paul had a genealogy, a background, and he knew he belonged.

3. "Of the tribe of Benjamin." This is like saying that he belonged to the best family. Benjamin had been the favorite son of old Jacob. Rachel had given birth to Benjamin when she died, and she had called him "son of my sorrow," but Jacob had named him "son of my right hand." Rachel had been the bright spot in his life before Peniel, and when he had looked in the crib at little Benjamin, he had seen him as Rachel's son. Benjamin became his right hand, his walking stick, the one on whom he leaned. Also the first king of Israel came from the tribe of Benjamin. His name was Saul, and I have a notion that Saul of Tarsus was named after him. So Paul could say with pride that he came from the tribe of Benjamin.

It is an advantage to be able to say, "My father was a minister of the Word of God," or, "My father was a layman who stood for the Word of God." On the other hand, sometimes it can work for a hindrance. I find people who say, "Dr. McGee, I was brought up in such-and-such a church; my grandfather was a founder of the church. There is even a window in the church dedicated to him. So I'll never leave that church." That can be a hindrance if the church has become liberal and the Word of God is no longer preached there. But for Paul, being of the tribe of Benjamin was a definite asset.

4. "An Hebrew of the Hebrews." This means he was a leader. He

was in the highest stratum of the religious circle. He was up at the top.

5. "As touching the law, a Pharisee." The Pharisees represented the very best in Israel. They were a religious-political party, and their aim was to establish the kingdom. They had arisen sometime after or during the Captivity. They were fundamental. They believed in the integrity of the Scriptures; they believed in angels; they believed in the resurrection and in miracles. They were also extremely nationalistic in their politics.

I think the reason they sent Nicodemus to see Jesus was because they thought, *Here is a prophet come out of Galilee. If he will just let us hitch our wagon to his star, we'll go places because we know how to manipulate Rome.* The Pharisees thought they could bring the kingdom by political manipulation. They wanted to establish the kingdom of God here upon this earth. Paul could say that he was a Pharisee.

6. "Concerning zeal, persecuting the church." Paul thought he was doing God's will when he persecuted the church. The other Pharisees were willing to relax when they had run the Christians out of Jerusalem, but Paul was determined to ferret them out all over the world. That was his purpose on his way to Damascus at the time of his conversion.

7. "Touching the righteousness which is in the law, blameless." Notice that he does not say he was sinless or perfect; he says he was blameless. In Romans 7:7 Paul tells us his story: ". . . I had not known sin, but by the law: for I had not known lust, except the law had said, Thou shalt not covet." Paul does not claim sinless perfection. This commandment showed him his sin.

Now if you break the commandment, "Thou shalt not steal," you'll have the evidence, or you may leave your fingerprints back at the scene of the crime. The same thing could be said about murder—you would have a *corpus delicti* on your hands. It is impossible to commit adultery without somebody else knowing about it. But you can covet and nobody would be the wiser. If Paul had kept quiet, we might think he had reached the place of sinless perfection, but he very frankly said he had not. He says that the Law "slew him."

What he means by "touching the righteousness which is in the law, blameless" is that he had brought the proper sacrifice for his sin to make things right before God. Paul was sincere. Regarding the Law, Paul was a supersaint. He had every right to say, "If any other man thinketh that he hath whereof he might trust in the flesh, I more."

These were the things that Paul had on the credit side of the ledger. It was such a big total that he felt all of these things commended him to God. He thought they were all credits to him.

On the debit side of his ledger was a Person he hated. That was Jesus Christ. Out of his hatred Paul was trying to eliminate the followers of Jesus Christ.

Then one day the Lord Jesus met Paul on the road to Damascus, and Paul changed his whole bookkeeping system. What had been a debit became a credit, and what he had considered a credit became a debit. It was a complete revolution.

But what things were gain to me, those I counted loss for Christ [Phil. 3:7].

On the credit side of the ledger Paul had been adding up his background and his character and his religion. It seemed like an impressive list—and it *was*, on the human plane. Suddenly it all became a debit—he no longer trusted in those things because he met Jesus Christ. He had hated Him before and was on the way to Damascus to persecute His followers, but now the One on the debit side was moved to the credit side. He put his entire trust in the Lord Jesus Christ.

Now, my friend, if the bookkeeping system of this country were transformed like that, it would upset the economy of the world. It would be a revolution. Actually, any conversion is a revolution because what things are gain become a loss, and loss becomes gain. It turns you upside down and right side up. It gets you in an altogether different position. That is what conversion is.

Now there is a time lapse between verses 7 and 8. I don't know the length of time, but I think it extends all the way through Paul's life from his conversion to the time he was writing this epistle. He had gone on his missionary journeys, and now he was in a prison in Rome.

Yea doubtless, and I count all things but loss for the excellency of the knowledge of Christ Jesus my Lord: for whom I have suffered the loss of all things, and do count them but dung, that I may win Christ [Phil. 3:8].

Paul's conversion was not just an experience of a moment. Conversion is not a balloon ascension. A great many people think that you can go down to some altar and have an experience, see a vision, and be carried to the heights—and that's it. Oh, my friend, conversion is something that stays with you. It is not for just a moment. Although it happens in a moment of time, it continues for a lifetime. And sanctification is not a great emotional experience; it is a daily walk in dependence upon God.

Paul says that since that moment of his conversion he lives for Christ. He has suffered the loss of all things. Jesus Christ is uppermost in his thinking. The things that he used to consider most precious he now considers to be *dung*—that is strong language! He says he flushes his religion down the drain. He flushes away all the things he used to trust. Now he trusts the Lord Jesus and Him *only* for his salvation.

I remember hearing Dr. Carroll say, "When I was converted, I lost my religion." A great many people need to lose their religion and find Jesus Christ as Paul did. He was so revolutionized that what had been his prized possession is now relegated to the garbage can!

Paul goes on with a theological statement of what happened to him.

And be found in him, not having mine own righteousness, which is of the law, but that which is through the faith of Christ, the righteousness which is of God by faith [Phil. 3:9].

This is the verse that came to John Bunyan as he walked through the cornfields one night, wondering how he could stand before God. He said that suddenly he saw himself—not just as a sinner, but as sin from the crown of his head to the soles of his feet. He realized that he had nothing, and that Christ had everything.

"Not having mine own righteousness"—his own righteousness, as he has made clear, is of the Law; that is, it is law-keeping. For example, he could boast of the fact that he kept the Sabbath day. But Paul now says to let no man judge you in respect of the Sabbath days (see Col. 2:16). My friend, I could boast of the fact that I preach so many times during the year and that I have a daily radio program, but these things count *nothing* for salvation. "Mine own righteousness" is a legal righteousness, and God has already declared that all our righteousnesses are as filthy rags in His sight (see Isa. 64:6), and God is just not taking in dirty laundry. However, He will take in dirty sinners, and He is the One who will clean them up.

Paul had given up his claim to all of his own righteousness.

When speaking at the Hollywood Christian group years ago, I recall a young couple who had been converted. They were talented kids and were really beautiful people. On the human side they had everything. They were called on to give a testimony before my message. They said that now that they had been converted they were going to use their wonderful talent for the Lord. So after I had finished teaching that night, I met with them over a cup of coffee. I said, "I have a question I would like to ask you that sort of bothers me. You made the statement that you have a wonderful talent to use for Jesus. I would like to know what it is. You danced in nightclubs, you sang in nightclubs, and you told stories in nightclubs. Do you think Jesus could use that?" Well, they said they hadn't thought of it like that. I said, "Look, when you come to Christ, you come as bankrupt sinners. You don't offer Him anything. You come with *nothing*. You are beggars. You have nothing; He has *everything*, and He offers it to you."

Oh, my friend, let's get this verse into our thinking! "Be found in him, not having mine own righteousness, which is of the law, but that which is through the faith of Christ, the righteousness which is of God by faith."

"By faith" is the important word. That is the only way in the world you can get it. You can't work for it; you can't buy it; you can't steal it. You just trust Him.

"The righteousness which is of God" came about because, when Christ died on the cross, He subtracted your sins, and He rose again from the dead for your justification, your *righteousness*. My friend, God can't even *stand* us in our unregenerate state. We are not attractive to Him! The very fact that He loved us and gave His Son for us is the most amazing statement ever made. We are accepted in the Beloved.

PAUL CHANGED HIS PURPOSE FOR THE PRESENT

Paul is no longer going to try to build up legal righteousness. He isn't going to see how religious and pious he can be or how much he can persecute the church. Since he has changed his bookkeeping system of the past, he is also going to change his purpose for the present. Listen to what he is going to do:

That I may know him, and the power of his resurrection, and the fellowship of his sufferings, being made conformable unto his death;

If by any means I might attain unto the resurrection of the dead [Phil. 3:10–11].

Some people get the impression that being saved by faith means there is no motivation for conduct and works. They think that if a person is saved by grace it must mean he just sits around and twiddles his thumbs. Nothing could be further from the truth. Saving faith is a faith that *moves* you. James said (and he is not talking about law-works but faith-works), ". . . shew me thy faith without thy works, and I will shew thee my faith by my works" (James 2:18). My friend, if you have been saved, I want to see your works. If you don't have works, you are not saved! That is exactly what Paul is saying. If you have been saved by faith you have a new motivation, a new life purpose, a new life-style. If your faith in Christ hasn't changed you, you haven't been saved. You are still the same old man producing the same old life. Paul dissipates any notion that being saved by faith means you can sit in a rocking chair and rock yourself all the way to heaven.

Paul exhibits an effort and an energy that is derived from the Holy Spirit, which is far greater than any legal effort. Under the Law, this man was willing to go to Damascus to stamp out the followers of

Christ. Under the grace-faith system, he will go to the end of the earth to make followers of Christ and to witness for Him. Faith produces something. Let us be perfectly clear about this. Your works have nothing to do with your salvation. You are shut up to a cross for salvation. God has only one question for the lost sinner to answer: "What will you do with Jesus who died for you?" If you will accept Him as your Savior, you are saved by faith. That is the righteousness that comes only by faith. Even your life after salvation doesn't build up a righteousness that has anything to do with your salvation. Your faith in Christ is a motivation for you to live for God. That is the reason Paul went on to live as he did.

I just do not understand people who are doing nothing for God. Some people say that they can't do anything. Well, to be very candid with you, you can help me or other Bible teachers get out the Word of God. I'm an old man, but I am not going to quit. I'm going to press toward the mark for the prize of the high calling of God. I have told God that if He would let me live, I'd get out His Word as long as I live. Oh, my friend, our faith in Christ gives a real motivation to work for Him!

"That I may know him"—Paul at the end of his life still had the ambition to know Christ. Today some saints give me the impression that they have complete knowledge and they only need to polish their halo every morning and are ready to take off at any moment. Yet Paul, the greatest missionary the world has ever seen, said at the end of his life, "My ambition is still to know Christ—His person and the power of His resurrection."

The greatest comfort in my life is the reality of Christ. I need the reality of Christ in my life—now don't point an accusing finger at me, because that's what you need also.

"And the fellowship of his sufferings"—oh, how we need to know the fellowship of His sufferings! I was moved to tears by a letter from someone who, after reading our message on Psalm 22, wrote, "Oh, I never knew how much Christ suffered for me!" My friend, I want to know the fellowship of His sufferings, I want to enter into them. To know Christ and His work of redemption will engage our attention for eternity. We are going to spend all eternity praising Him for that. If you are bored with it now, if you don't enjoy praising Christ now, I don't know why you should want to go to heaven.

"If by any means I might attain unto the resurrection of the dead." When Paul uses the word *if* he is not expressing a doubt about his participation in the Rapture. Rather, he is affirming that he will have part in it with great *joy*. Paul did not expect to attain perfection in this life; therefore, he wanted to have full participation in the coming Rapture. When someone tells me that he does not believe in the Rapture, I wonder about his relationship to the person of Christ. Paul is saying, "My ambition, the thing I'm moving toward, is not only that I might know Him but that I might have a meaningful, joyous part in the 'out-resurrection,' which is the rapture of the church." The Old Testament saints are not to be raised until the end of the Great Tribulation Period (see Dan. 12:1–3). The rest of the dead will not be raised until the end of the Millennium.

Have you ever stopped to think what the coming of Christ really means? Most of us think, "Boy, it will get us out of this old world." Paul says, "It will get me into His presence."

> **Not as though I had already attained, either were already perfect: but I follow after, if that I may apprehend that for which also I am apprehended of Christ Jesus [Phil. 3:12].**

The knowledge that he will not attain perfection does not deter Paul from moving in that direction. Perfection means complete maturity. Paul knew he had not arrived. He certainly agreed with Peter that we should ". . . grow in grace, and in the knowledge of our Lord and Saviour Jesus Christ . . ." (2 Pet. 3:18).

Now the next verse will give us the *modus operandi* of the life of Paul:

> **Brethren, I count not myself to have apprehended: but this one thing I do, forgetting those things which are behind, and reaching forth unto those things which are before [Phil. 3:13].**

"I count not myself to have apprehended"—Paul is saying that he hadn't arrived. Oh, so many saints feel comfortable in their ignorance. They think they know it all.

"This one thing I do." Talk about the simple life—if we could get the Christian life down to where we should have it, it would really be an uncomplicated life. Paul had whittled his life down to one point.

"Forgetting those things which are behind." He is leaving the past behind with all his mistakes, not letting it handicap him for the future. The future—he lives in the present in the anticipation of the future when he will grow and develop. (Someone has well said that today is the tomorrow you worried about yesterday.)

I press toward the mark for the prize of the high calling of God in Christ Jesus [Phil. 3:14].

"I press toward the mark for the prize." Paul likens himself to a track star, running for a prize. We must remember that Paul had witnessed the Olympic Games—at least, he had every opportunity to do so. There was a great amphitheater in Ephesus which seated one hundred thousand people, and the Olympic Games were held there at times. Paul was living in Ephesus for three years, and it is difficult for me to believe that he hadn't seen the games, especially since he used so many figures of speech that were taken from those athletic events.

"The prize of the high calling of God in Christ Jesus"—the prize is not some earthly reward but it is to be caught up and be in the presence of Christ. "The high calling of God" is sometimes translated "the upward call of God." We are going to be in His presence. We are going to be like Him. These are things that Paul says are out yonder in the future for him.

Now let's be clear on one thing: we don't run for salvation. Salvation is not the prize. Either we have Christ or we don't have Him. We either trust Him or we don't trust Him. The only way we can have salvation is through faith in Christ. It is a gift. A gift is different from a prize. The wonderful folk on our radio staff presented me with a birthday gift. Somebody said, "We have a gift for you, Dr. McGee," and handed a box to me. I believed them and I took it. I didn't put my hands behind my back and say, "Well, I'm not sure you really mean business. I am not sure that you intend to do this for me." I just accepted it and thanked them for it. I didn't have to run a race to win it; I didn't have to work for it. It was a gift. "For by grace are ye saved through faith; and that not of yourselves: it is the gift of God; Not of works, lest any man should boast" (Eph. 2:8–9). Salvation is not won at a race. Salvation is a gift which is accepted.

Now Paul, after receiving eternal life, is out running for a prize. Christ became everything to him, and he is running a race that he might win Christ. In what way? Well, someday he is going to appear in His presence. His whole thought is: "When I come into His presence, I don't want to be ashamed." John said that it is possible to be ashamed at His appearing: "And now, little children, abide in him, that, when he shall appear, we may have confidence, and not be ashamed before him at his coming" (1 John 2:28). There are a great many Christians today talking about wishing Christ would come, who, if they really knew what it will mean to them, would probably like to postpone it for a while. If you think that you can live a careless Christian life and not have to answer for it, you are entirely wrong. One of these days you will have to stand before the judgment seat of Christ to give an account of the way you lived your life. I suggest that you get down on the racecourse and start living for Him.

Let us therefore, as many as be perfect, be thus minded: and if in any thing ye be otherwise minded, God shall reveal even this unto you [Phil. 3:15].

"As many as be perfect"—what does he mean by that? I think I can illustrate this by my orange trees. My three orange trees are loaded with fruit this year. Some of the oranges are still green, but for this particular time of year, they are perfect. They are perfect oranges. But if you come and see me in a month, they will not be perfect oranges if they stay just like they are now. You see, when Paul says "perfect," he means arriving where one should be in maturation. Another illustration would be that of a baby. Suppose we have a baby here seventeen months old. My, what a wonderful baby he is—he wins a blue ribbon.

But if you see him seventeen years later and he is still saying, "Da-da," there is something radically wrong. Maturation is the thought Paul has in mind. He is saying this: "Let us, therefore, as many as are complete in Christ, who are growing normally in Christ, let us be thus minded." In other words, have the same mind as Paul. Get out on the racetrack with Paul and press on toward the same goal.

"And if in any thing ye be otherwise minded, God shall reveal even this unto you." Maybe you have some other idea, and maybe God does have something else for you to do. If you are willing to do it, He will show it to you. God is able to lead a *willing* believer. You may remember that the psalmist told us not to be like the horse and the mule that must have a bridle in his mouth in order to be led. If God must lead you around like that, it will hurt. Why not let Him lead you by His eye? That is the way He would like to do it. This is what Paul is talking about—"God shall reveal even this unto you." God will reveal His will to you if you want to be led. I hear Christians say, "If only I knew the will of God." It's a matter of being in touch with the Lord Jesus Christ. It is a matter of drawing close to Him. It is a willingness to do His will when He shows it to you. There is no little formula for discovering the will of God. One cannot live a careless life and expect a vision or an angel or some green light to appear to show the way to go in a crisis. Knowing the will of God comes through a day-by-day walk with Him and a willingness to be led by Him. This will keep you on the right route through life, and it will be a great joy to your heart.

> **Nevertheless, whereto we have already attained, let us walk by the same rule, let us mind the same thing [Phil. 3:16].**

Paul is encouraging the Philippian believers to get out on the racetrack. He wants them to press on for the prize—the high calling of God in Christ Jesus.

Then he goes on to give himself as an example.

> **Brethren, be followers together of me, and mark them which walk so as ye have us for an ensample [Phil. 3:17].**

I wish I could say that. I can't, but Paul could. He says, "If you want to know how to do it, watch me." This is not to be an imitation. What he means is that you learn to share the power of Christ in the body of Christ, the church.

I believe it is proper for a believer to function within a Christian organization, a church. It doesn't have to be a building with a tall steeple on it. Many folk think they must go to a certain type of building. That is not necessary. You can function within a Christian organization. My feeling is that if there is a good Bible church in your community where the Word of God is given out, you are out of the will of God if you are not identified with it. If there is a good Christian organization in your town through which God is working, and you are not supporting it, I think you are out of the will of God. This, I believe, is what Paul means here and what he says elsewhere.

Now Paul discusses the negative side.

(For many walk, of whom I have told you often, and now tell you even weeping, that they are the enemies of the cross of Christ:

Whose end is destruction, whose God is their belly, and whose glory is in their shame, who mind earthly things.) [Phil. 3:18–19].

This is as severe a condemnation as you can find of those who profess to be Christians. They claim to be Christians, yet they contradict their profession by their lives. Their God is their belly—that's an awful thing! This means that they are led by their appetites. Some professing Christians have an appetite for money. They will do most anything for the almighty dollar. Others have such an appetite for sex that it becomes actually their god. Others covet—that is the cause of much of the strife and vainglory. The basic cause of it is that they have their hearts and minds on earthly things. They live for self and self only, and they actually glory in this. They are proud of what they should be ashamed.

Paul is saying that if you have trusted Christ, if you have had that kind of revolution that happened to him on the Damascus road, if Christ is the all-absorbing thinking of your mind and your time and your talent and your possessions, then this will tell in your life. James put it like this: "Even so faith, if it hath not works, is dead, being alone. Yea, a man may say, Thou hast faith, and I have works: shew me thy faith without thy works, and I will shew thee my faith by my works" (James 2:17–18). In other words, my friend, if you haven't any works you are not going to convince your neighbor. He will judge your faith by your works. As Calvin said, "Faith alone saves, but the faith that saves is not alone." Some folk feel that the statement "whose God is their belly" is crude. Well, the statement is not crude, but the condition it speaks of is certainly crude. How tragic it is to see Christians who are given over to the passing things of this world, who "mind earthly things."

PAUL CHANGED HIS HOPE FOR THE FUTURE

For our conversation is in heaven; from whence also we look for the Saviour, the Lord Jesus Christ [Phil. 3:20].

A better translation for "conversation" is citizenship. It means the total way of life; it means a new life-style. An even better translation is that made by Mrs. Montgomery: "For our city home is in heaven." Probably that is closer to what Paul is saying. The Greek word for "conversation" is politeuō, meaning "to act as a citizen." The city of Philippi was a Roman colony. In Philippi the laws of Rome were enforced. The people wore the same kind of styles that were worn in Rome. They spoke Latin. Everything in Philippi was like Rome because it was a colonial city.

Today, believers, collectively called the church, should be a colony of heaven, and they ought to act like they act in heaven and speak the language of heaven. Unfortunately, this is not always the case, but it should be our goal. Paul is saying that we are ambassadors of Christ here on this earth; we are to represent heaven and heaven's message here upon earth today, because "our citizenship is in heaven."

"From whence also we look for the Saviour, the Lord Jesus Christ."

Paul expresses the hope of the believer on the high plane of praise to God. It is the joyful anticipation of His return.

The hope of the believer in the New Testament is never the Great Tribulation Period. After he says our citizenship is in heaven, he says that from there "we look for the Saviour, the Lord Jesus Christ." He doesn't say anything about going through the Great Tribulation Period, which will be a time of judgment, and the church is delivered from judgment. Believers will not go through the Great Tribulation any more than Enoch went through the Flood. Many folk maintain that the Lord can preserve the church through the Great Tribulation. Yes, He can; God kept Noah in a boat through the Flood, but He took Enoch out of the world. There will be two groups of people who will be His during the Great Tribulation Period. One will be taken out, as He says to the church in Philadelphia: "Because thou hast kept the word of my patience, I also will keep thee from the hour of temptation, which shall come upon all the world, to try them that dwell upon the earth" (Rev. 3:10). The other group will be going through the Great Tribulation. There will be a great company of Gentiles and there will be 144,000 of Israel who will go through the Great Tribulation Period because they are to be sealed by God.

Let me digress to say that the teaching that the church is to go through the Great Tribulation is becoming increasingly absurd to me. The advocates of this theory maintain that there is not a verse in Scripture that says the church will not go through the Great Tribulation. While it is true that it doesn't say it in those words, neither is there a verse in Scripture that has anything to say about the church not doing other things. For instance, I am confident that we are all going to have a position, a job to do, throughout eternity, but Scripture does not go into detail on that sort of thing. However, Scripture is very clear on the fact that the church has a glorious, wonderful hope for the future. It seems to many of us that it is tissue-thin between where we are now and the Rapture of the church. However, Scripture does not tell us when Christ will come. Apparently Paul felt that during his lifetime the Lord could come, and there is no record of Paul's expecting to first go through the Great Tribulation. He experienced a lot of trouble during his life, but he never interpreted that as the Great Tribulation.

With a note of glad expectancy Paul says, "For our conversation [citizenship] is in heaven; from whence also we look for the Saviour, the Lord Jesus Christ"—*after* we go through the real Tribulation? It doesn't say that in my Bible. Nowhere does it say the church is going through the Great Tribulation, my friend. Paul's joyful expectancy makes it very clear that he was looking for Christ's return, *not* for the Great Tribulation.

Who shall change our vile body, that it may be fashioned like unto his glorious body, according to the working whereby he is able even to subdue all things unto himself [Phil. 3:21].

"Our vile body" might be better translated "body of humiliation" or "body of corruption." It means that He shall change our earthly body. This body that we have is an earthly body, subject to all kinds of limitations. It is adapted to this earth. We are not naturally equipped to go up into space. Our bodies are earthly bodies.

"That it may be fashioned like unto his glorious body." These bodies are corruptible bodies. One of these days you and I will move out of these bodies. We will leave them because they are corruptible. They are going to be changed—I'd like to trade mine in right now— "fashioned like unto his glorious body." It will be a body like the one the Lord Jesus had after His resurrection. It will be a glorified body. Paul speaks of it in his letter to the Corinthians: "Behold, I shew you a mystery; We shall not all sleep, but we shall all be changed, In a moment, in the twinkling of an eye, at the last trump . . ." (1 Cor. 15:51–52). The point is that it will be sudden—when the trumpet shall sound.

While I am dealing with misinterpretations of this passage, let me say that some folk assume that one of the angels spoken of in the Book of Revelation is to blow this trumpet. However, the one blowing the trumpet is not indicated here. The Book of Revelation deals with Israel. In the Old Testament we read that Israel was moved on the wilderness march by the blowing of two silver trumpets. Israel is accustomed to trumpets; we are not. Perhaps you are remembering that the "last trump" is mentioned in connection with the Rapture in 1 Thessalonians: "For the Lord himself shall descend from heaven with a shout, with the voice of the archangel, and with the trump of God . . ." (1 Thess. 4:16). Notice it is the trump of God. Whoever turned it over to Gabriel and said Gabriel will blow his horn? I question if Gabriel even owns a horn. It is the Lord who will descend with the voice of an archangel and the trump of God. Both speak of the dignity and the majesty of that shout of His. His voice will be penetrating and awe-inspiring. Listen to the way John describes the voice of the glorified Christ: "I was in the Spirit on the Lord's day, and heard behind me a great voice, as of a trumpet" (Rev. 1:10). And when he turned to see who was speaking, he saw the glorified Christ. It was His voice that John heard. There are no trumpets connected with the church.

Today Christ's word to us is this: "Behold, I stand at the door, and knock: if any man hear my voice, and open the door, I will come in to him, and will sup with him, and he with me" (Rev. 3:20). It is His invitation to the evening meal—the last call for dinner. It is an invitation to come to Him before the night of the Great Tribulation falls. When the door is opened, there will go from this earth a group of people who have been put on the launching pad of faith—and they won't go through the Great Tribulation Period. May I say to you that those who expect the church to go through the Tribulation have, in my judgment, the flimsiest theory that is abroad, yet there are many intelligent men who hold this view. However, I find that these men spend more time with philosophy and psychology and history and related subjects than they do with the study of the Word of God.

"Who shall change our vile body, that it may be fashioned like unto his glorious body." This is exactly the same thought that John had: "Beloved, now are we the sons of God, and it doth not yet appear what we shall be: but we know that, when he shall appear, we shall be like him; for we shall see him as he is" (1 John 3:2). Christ hasn't appeared yet, but when He appears, we shall be like Him. Notice the high hope, the expectancy and excitement, the great anticipation of Christ's return. (There is not the slightest suggestion that either Paul or John expected to first go through the Great Tribulation Period.)

Paul had a hope for the future. What is your hope for the future? The Great Tribulation Period? My friend, if that is your prospect, you are about as hopeless as the man who has no hope!

Taking a trip recently to the Hawaiian Islands, instead of flying the direct route, we came in from the north. The reason the pilot gave us was that there was a storm front on the southern route, and he skirted it, although it made us about thirty minutes late. I appreciated the fact that he went around the storm. It used to be that a pilot would say, "There is a storm front ahead of us, and we are going to have turbulence for the next thirty minutes." I didn't look forward to that—it was no blessed hope for me! But it surely is nice to have him say we are taking another route so we will miss the storm. And the Lord says to the church, "We're going to miss the storm, the Great Tribulation." My friend, you can twist it around to suit your own theory, but that is what He says. "For our conversation is in heaven; from whence also we look for the Saviour, the Lord Jesus Christ." That was Paul's hope for the future, and it is our hope.

CHAPTER 4

THEME: Power for Christian living; joy—the source of power; prayer—the secret of power; contemplation of Christ—the sanctuary of power; in Christ—the satisfaction of power

We have seen the *philosophy* of Christian living, the *pattern* for Christian living, the prize for Christian living, and now we shall see the *power* for Christian living. All the others would be meaningless and useless if there were no power for them. A philosophy of life is no good unless there is power to carry it out. A pattern is no good unless there is power supplied to have that pattern in our own lives. A prize is no good if we cannot achieve the goal. Therefore, power is all important.

I would think one of the reasons that the Spirit of God did not let Paul end this epistle when he wrote in 3:1, "Finally, my brethren," was because He wanted to let us know today that there is *power* for Christian living. We need to know that we can do all things through Christ who strengthens us.

We will find in this chapter that joy is the *source* of power; prayer is the *secret* of power; and contemplation of Christ is the *sanctuary* of power.

JOY—THE SOURCE OF POWER

Therefore, my brethren dearly beloved and longed for, my joy and crown, so stand fast in the Lord, my dearly beloved [Phil. 4:1].

"My joy and crown"—you see, they were going to be in the presence of Christ someday, and Paul expected to receive a *crown* for winning these folks to the Lord. Also they were his *joy* down here. Oh, how he loved these believers in Philippi!

"So stand fast in the Lord, my dearly beloved." And, as Paul said to the Ephesian believers, ". . . take unto you the whole armour of God, that ye may be able to withstand in the evil day, and having done all, to stand" (Eph. 6:13). The Christian faith will produce stability of life.

I beseech Euodias, and beseech Syntyche, that they be of the same mind in the Lord [Phil. 4:2].

Now he comes to the only problem in the Philippian church. There was a ripple on the surface, but it was not serious. Paul doesn't even mention it until near the end of his letter. Apparently these two ladies were not speaking to each other. We have already seen this when he admonished the Philippian believers to be of the same mind in the Lord. He did not mean they must be carbon copies of each other. They may have differences of opinion about many different things, but that will not separate two people who have the mind of Christ. It is one of the glorious truths about the body of Christ that each member can be different and yet all are one in Christ.

And I entreat thee also, true yokefellow, help those women which laboured with me in the gospel, with Clement also, and with other my fellow-labourers whose names are in the book of life [Phil. 4:3].

It is apparent that women occupied a prominent place in the early church, and for a woman to be prominent was unusual in that day.

Now that I am no longer a pastor I can say this (I always said it reluctantly or very carefully before): I believe that the reason women become preachers is because women have not been given their proper place in the church. The office of deaconess, even if it exists in the church, is treated very lightly. I believe that is an important office and should be recognized as such. The more I study the Word of God, the more I am convinced of this. Paul plainly said that "those women . . . laboured with me in the gospel."

"With Clement also"—here is a believer over in Philippi whom we haven't met before.

"With other my fellow-labourers"—apparently there was a great company of believers in Philippi "whose names are in the book of life." That was the important thing: their names are in the Book of Life.

Rejoice in the Lord alway: and again I say, Rejoice [Phil. 4:4].

This is a commandment to a Christian, a believer. Rejoice in the Lord always. That means regardless of the day, whether it is dark or bright, whether it is difficult or easy, whether it brings problems and temptations or clear sailing on cloud nine. We are commanded to rejoice. He repeats it, in case we missed it the first time: "again I say, Rejoice." Joy is something we cannot produce ourselves; it is a fruit of the Holy Spirit.

There is no power in a Christian's life if he has no joy. One who does not experience the joy of the Lord has no power at all.

After Nehemiah had finished building the wall of Jerusalem, they set up a pulpit at the Water Gate, and there Ezra read from the Scriptures from morning until midday. These people had come out of captivity in Babylon. Most of them had never in their lives heard the Word of God. It overwhelmed them. They began to mourn and to weep. So Nehemiah said, "Wait a minute—you're not to weep! This is a great day. You are to share in the blessings, the physical blessings, that God has given to you, and God wants you to enjoy them." God has given to us richly all things to enjoy, and to enjoy means to rejoice. That's your strength, that's your power. You can't be a Christian with power without joy—that's what gets up the steam. Joy is the source of power.

Let me illustrate this because it is something that the world has taken over. In fact, the commercial world has made it rather hypocritical. A successful salesman is a very happy fellow. You have never gone into a store to buy something and had the salesperson weep on your shoulder when you asked about a certain product! Of course not. He begins to smile and say how wonderful the item is. How far would the Fuller brush man get if he were a sad little fellow who went around weeping at every door? Believe me, he doesn't use that approach.

The Fuller brush man calls at our house on Saturdays. He is not a sorrowful fellow by any means. I don't know whether he is having trouble at home or not, but he sure radiates joy. One Saturday morning my wife had gone to the market, and from my study window I saw him coming. I thought, *I'll ignore him because I'm busy, and I'm not going to fool with brushes today.* So he came and pushed the doorbell. I let him push it. He pushed it two or three times. I thought, *He'll leave now.* But he didn't leave. He knew somebody was in the house, so he just put his thumb down on the doorbell and held it. Finally in self-defense I had to go to the door. When I opened the door, I expected him to be a little irritated because I had made him wait. But no, he was happy about it. Everything pleased him. He greeted me joyfully, "Dr. McGee, I didn't expect to see you today!" With a scowl I said, "My wife has gone to the market. She'll see you the next time you are around." But that wasn't enough for him. I do not know how he did it, but in the next ten seconds he was in the living room and I was holding a little brush in my hand. Then I couldn't order him out—he'd given me a little brush. And so I stood there listening to his sales pitch. When he had finished, I said, "Now look, I don't buy brushes and I don't need one. My wife generally buys from you, and she'll probably buy next time, but I haven't time to look at them. I'm busy this morning." So he thanked me and started down the walkway *whistling!* You would have thought I had bought every brush he had! I met a man who trains Fuller brush salesmen, and I told him about this experience. He said that they were so instructed; they are trained to radiate joy.

Now I do not know if that Fuller brush man was happy or not, but a child of God ought to have *real* joy, the joy of the Lord, in his life.

The world spends a great deal of money trying to produce joy, which they call happiness. Comedians are millionaires because they tell a few funny stories. People shell out the money to hear them. Why? Because they want to laugh. They are trying to find a little happiness as they go through life. The child of God who goes through life with a sour look and a jaundiced approach to this world will never have any power in his life. "Rejoice in the Lord alway: and again I say, Rejoice."

The world tries to work up joy in another way. They call it the *happy hour* or *attitude adjustment hour*. They spend a couple of hours drinking and hope it will help them overcome the problems of life and give them a little happiness. I have watched the folk who go in there, and none of them look happy when they go in. In an hour or two when they come out, I can't see that there has been any improvement. But they have had a "happy hour." A great many people are trying to compensate for the inadequacies in their own lives in that manner.

I have thought it would be nice if churches could have an *attitude adjustment hour*. Here comes Mrs. Brown. She has just heard some choice gossip during the week, and she can hardly wait to spread it around in the church. Wouldn't it be wonderful to take her into an attractive room and have a cup of coffee with her and get her into a sweet mood of rejoicing in the Lord so she would not go around spreading her gossip? Here comes Deacon Jones, breathing fire like a dragon because something doesn't suit him. It would be nice to take him to that room and help him recover his cool so he could go in and enjoy the sermon. We need an attitude adjustment hour, a happy hour, in the church. Frankly, the Devil has gotten in his licks—he has made folk believe they can't have fun going to church, and I think they can. I think it ought to be a joyful place and a place of power.

Sometimes prayer meetings are called the hour of power. Well, that is nice, but we need to get back to the *source* of the power, which is joy. In our prayer meetings, before we ask God for something else, let's pray that He'll give us joy in our lives. There was a little song we used to sing at summer Bible schools (which I used to conduct as a young preacher) with these words:

> Down in the dumps I'll never go;
> That's where the Devil keeps me low.

That song has a sound theological message, because this is exactly what the Devil tries to do. He attempts to take away our joy because it is the source of power.

PRAYER—THE SECRET OF POWER

**Let your moderation be known unto all men. The Lord is
at hand [Phil. 4:5].**

Matthew Arnold, in one of his delightful essays, interprets it this
way: "Let your sweet reasonableness be known unto all men." I like
that. We need to be reasonable believers, not bigots in our faith. Of
course we ought to have deep convictions, but we should not be given
to bigotry or riding a hobbyhorse—always emphasizing some little
point. What we need to do is emphasize the big point—we do have
one—the big point is the person of Christ. If we are going to ride a
hobbyhorse, let Him be the hobbyhorse. "Let your sweet reasonableness be known unto all men."

"The Lord is at hand." Paul believed that the Lord Jesus would
come at any moment. He was not expecting to enter the Great Tribulation; he says, "The Lord is at hand." That's quite wonderful!

**Be careful for nothing; but in every thing by prayer and
supplication with thanksgiving let your requests be
made known unto God [Phil. 4:6].**

"Be careful for nothing" is sometimes translated: Be anxious for nothing, or not overly anxious. The fact of the matter is that Paul seems to
be making a play upon two indefinite pronouns: nothing and everything. Let me give you my translation, which I call the McGee-icus Ad
Absurdum. It goes like this: "Worry about nothing; pray about everything." Prayer is the secret of power.

"Worry about nothing." In verse 4 we were given one of the new
commandments God has given us: Rejoice. Now here is another commandment: Worry about nothing; pray about everything.

Nothing is a very interesting word. If you have something, it's not
nothing—that is not correct grammar, but it is an accurate statement.
Nothing is nothing, and you are to worry about nothing. Does this
mean we are to look at life through rose-colored glasses, that we are
not to face reality? Are we to believe that sin is not real, that sickness

is not real, that problems are not real? Are we to ignore these things? No. Paul says that we are to worry about nothing because we are to pray about everything. *Nothing* is the most exclusive word in the English language. It leaves out everything. "Worry about *nothing*." I confess that this is a commandment I sometimes break—I worry.

But the reason we are to worry about nothing is because we are to pray about everything. This means that we are to talk to the Lord about everything in our lives. Nothing should be left out. Some years ago, I am told, a dowager in Philadelphia came to Dr. G. Campbell Morgan with this question, "Dr. Morgan, do you think we should pray about the *little* things in our lives?" Dr. Morgan in his characteristically British manner said, "Madam, can you mention anything in your life that is *big* to God?" When we say that we take our big problems to God, what do we mean? They are all little stuff to Him. And what we call little He wants us to bring to Him also. As believers we need to get in the habit of bringing everything to Him in prayer—nothing excluded. When I go on a trip in my car and it involves several hours of driving, I invite the Lord Jesus to go along with me. I talk to Him and tell Him everything about Vernon McGee, things I wouldn't tell you or anyone else. I tell Him everything. I think we ought to learn to do that. We ought to pray about everything.

Let me share with you an admonition by Fenelon, one of the mystics of the Middle Ages, which seems to encompass what Paul meant when he said, "Pray about everything."

> Tell God all that is in your heart, as one unloads one's heart, its pleasures and its pains, to a dear friend. Tell Him your troubles, that He may comfort you; tell Him your joys, that He may sober them; tell Him your longings, that He may purify them; tell Him your dislikes, that He may help you to conquer them; talk to Him of your temptations, that He may shield you from them; show Him the wounds of your heart, that He may heal them; lay bare your indifference to good, your depraved tastes for evil, your instability. Tell Him how self-love makes you unjust to others, how vanity tempts you to be insincere, how pride disguises you to yourself as to others.

> If you thus pour out all your weaknesses, needs, troubles, there will be no lack of what to say. You will never exhaust the subject. It is continually being renewed. People who have no secrets from each other never want subjects of conversation. They do not weigh their words, for there is nothing to be held back; neither do they seek for something to say. They talk out of the abundance of the heart, without consideration, just what they think. Blessed are they who attain to such familiar, unreserved intercourse with God.

For many years I have carried this quotation in my Bible, and every now and then I take it out and read it.

Maybe you think it sounds very pious when I am willing to testify that I take my burdens to the Lord in prayer. I must confess that after I spread everything out before Him, when I finish praying, I pick it all right back up, put the problems back on my shoulders, and start out with the burden again. That is my problem. The Lord wants us to trust Him so that we worry about nothing, pray about everything. I wish I could say to you that I'm as free as the bird in the trees, free as the bees gathering honey. That's the way He wants us to be.

We have a mockingbird in our yard. He gets my fruit, but I feel it is right for me to pay him something for the song he sings for me in the night. Now, actually, he isn't singing for me. I don't think he cares much whether I hear him or not. But he has a mate sitting on some eggs, and it would be a pretty boring job to sit on a bunch of eggs. So this mockingbird sings to his wife all during the night. The other morning I awakened around two o'clock, and my, how he was singing to her! How lovely. While sitting outside on my patio I noticed this mockingbird. He looked at me with disdain, flew right over to my apricot tree and started to eat apricots. He never asked me for permission to eat. He is free. He doesn't worry about finding something to eat. He knows those apricots will be there for him. My friend, do we really trust God like that? Worry about nothing and pray about everything.

"With thanksgiving let your requests be made known unto God." Paul never lets prayer become a leap in the dark. It rests on a foundation. "So then faith cometh by hearing, and hearing by the Word of God" (Rom. 10:17). Prayer rests on faith, and faith rests on the Word of God. Now he says that when you go to God with a request, thank Him Thank Him right then and there.

I know some commentators who interpret this to mean that when you get your answer to your prayer, you are to go back and thank God. Well, that's not what Paul said. Paul was able to express himself in the most versatile language which has ever been in the world, the Greek language, and he was able to say what he wanted to say. What he says is that when you make your requests, right there and then you are to thank God for hearing and answering your prayer.

Now perhaps you are thinking, *But maybe God won't answer my prayer. I have many unanswered prayers.* My Christian friend, I do not believe that you have unanswered prayers, and I think you ought to be ashamed of yourself for saying that you have a heavenly Father who won't hear and answer your prayers. You may have prayed for a certain thing and didn't get it, but you did get an answer to your prayer.

Let me illustrate this with a very homely illustration. My dad was not a Christian, but he was a good dad. He ran a cotton gin, and the machine would always be running. I would go in there when I was a little fellow and ask for a nickel for candy. He would reach down in his pocket and give me a nickel. One time I asked him for a bicycle. He said he couldn't afford it, and the answer was "No." I can tell you today that I never made a request of him that he didn't hear and answer. Most of the time the answer was no. Actually, my dad's *no* was more positive than his *yes*. His *no* ended the discussion. In fact, I have never understood young folk today who keep on arguing with their parents after the parents have handed down a decision. When my dad said, "No," that was the end of the discussion. I have learned now that the wise reply to most of my requests was no, although I did not think so at the time. But the fact is that he gave an answer to my every request.

God has a lot of spoiled children. When He says no to them, they pout and say, "I have unanswered prayers." You don't have unanswered prayers. God always hears and answers your prayers.

You can take anything to God in prayer, the big things and the little things. How can you sort them out? They are all little things to God. Let me give you another homely illustration. At the time of the building of the Panama Canal, after two or three failures, when the successful project was under way they wanted to go right through with it, and so the crew had no vacations. To compensate for it, the workers' families were sent down to be with them. So a certain young engineer, his wife and little son were sent down. Because of the danger of malaria, they were put out on a houseboat. Every afternoon that young engineer could be seen rowing himself out to the houseboat. One evening he had those long blueprints all spread out while his little son with his toy wagon was playing at his feet. Suddenly the child began to cry. A wheel had come off his wagon. The little fellow had worked with it and tried his best to put it back, but it was a hopeless project for him. Now would you think that the dad would shush him and put him out of the room—maybe tell the mother to come and get him because he was disturbing his work? No. He just laid aside the blueprints of that great canal, picked up his little boy and asked him what was the matter. The youngster held up his wagon in one hand and the wheel in the other. The father took the wheel and put it on the wagon with just one twist of the wrist. He kissed away the little fellow's tears and put him back on the floor where he played happily. He was a good father.

Now, my friend, it is God who put that father instinct deep down in the human heart of man because He is a compassionate Father. When a wheel comes off your wagon, it may look like an impossible problem to you, but He will hear and answer your cry. If He says no, it is because that is the best answer you could have. After I lost my human father, I lived several years before I turned to God and found that I had a heavenly Father. I learned that I can go to Him with my requests, and He answers me, as my human father used to do. And many times His answers are no.

When I was a young pastor in Texas, just married, I went to a certain city to candidate in a church. It was considered a strategic, outstanding church. After I'd preached twice that Sunday, I was given a call by the church. Then later they had to come back and tell me that the denomination would not permit them to call me. As I said, it was a strategic church and they needed a church politician there—which I was not. I didn't go into the ministry for that purpose. But I felt that the Lord had made a great mistake by not letting me go to that church as pastor. Several years ago Mrs. McGee and I went by that church just to see it. It had gone into liberalism. Things have happened there that I'll not mention. I said to her, "Do you remember years ago when I thought I should have had the call for that church?" She said, "Yes." Then I said, "I thank God that He heard and answered my prayer the *right* way—not the way I prayed it." I can look back and remember how I had cried to the Lord. I told Him how He had failed me and caused me to miss the greatest opportunity I ever had. Oh, I blamed Him, and I found fault with Him, and I actually scolded Him because He didn't seem to know what was the best for me! He had shut that door so tight that the resounding slam was in my ears for several years after that. My friend, my heavenly Father had answered my prayer, and I am ashamed of the fact that I did not thank Him at the time. My advice to you is this: Instead of saying that God has not answered your prayers, say, "My heavenly Father heard my prayer, but He told me no, which was the right answer." We are to let our "requests be made known unto God *with thanksgiving.*"

And the peace of God, which passeth all understanding, shall keep your hearts and minds through Christ Jesus [Phil. 4:7].

The Scripture speaks of other kinds of peace which we can understand. There is *world peace*. We have the assurance that someday peace will cover the earth as the waters cover the sea. It will come through the person of Christ, the Prince of Peace. Also there is the peace that comes when *sins are forgiven*. "Therefore being justified by faith, we have peace with God through our Lord Jesus Christ" (Rom. 5:1). Then there is the peace that is *tranquility*. The Lord Jesus said, "Peace I leave with you, my peace I give unto you . . ." (John 14:27). That is a marvelous peace, but it is not "the peace . . . which passeth all understanding." I do not know how to tell you this, but I do know it is a peace in which we do not live at all times. I think it is a peace that sweeps over our souls at certain times. I stood on the big island of Hawaii and looked out at a sunset with Mauna Kea, that great snow-capped mountain out there in the tropics, in the foreground. As I looked at the majesty of God's creation, what a peace came to me. I can't tell you what it was—it "passeth all understanding." And that same peace came when my heavenly Father let me have cancer. I went to the hospital frightened to death, and then that night I committed it all to Him and told Him I wanted to know *He* was real. He made Himself real and that peace that "passeth all understanding" flooded my soul. I don't know how to tell you what it is; I can only say that it is wonderful.

This peace "shall keep your hearts and minds through Christ Jesus." There are those who say that prayer changes things. I can't argue with that; prayer *does* change things. But that is not the primary purpose of prayer.

Notice that we entered this passage in anxiety, with worry, and we came out of the passage with peace. Between the two was prayer. Have things changed? Not really. The storm may still be raging, the waves still rolling high, the thunder still resounding. Although the storm has not abated, something has happened in the individual. Something has happened to the human soul and the human mind. In our anxiety we want God to change everything around us. "Give us this." "Don't let this happen." "Open up this door." We should be praying, "Oh, God, change *me*." Prayer is the secret of power. We enter with worry, we can come out in peace.

Joy is the *source* of power; prayer is the *secret* of power.

CONTEMPLATION OF CHRIST—THE SANCTUARY OF POWER

Finally, brethren, whatsoever things are true, whatsoever things are honest, whatsoever things are just, whatsoever things are pure, whatsoever things are lovely, whatsoever things are of good report; if there be any virtue, and if there be any praise, think on these things [Phil. 4:8].

"Finally, brethren"—remember that he said, "Finally, my brethren" at the beginning of chapter 3, when he was just halfway through? Well, now he is nearly through and is giving his last admonitions.

This has been called the briefest biography of Christ. He is the One who is "true." He is the Way, the Truth, and the Life. "Whatsoever things are honest"—He is honest. "Whatsoever things are just"—He is called the Just One. "Pure"—the only pure individual who ever walked this earth was the Lord Jesus. He asked the question, "Which of you convicteth me of sin?" No one did. He also said, ". . . the prince of this world cometh, and hath nothing in me" (John 14:30). Satan always finds something he can hook onto in me. How about you? But there was nothing in the Lord Jesus. He was ". . . holy, harmless, undefiled, separate from sinners . . ." (Heb. 7:26). He was *lovely* which means "gracious." *Virtue* has to do with strength and courage. He was the One of courage, a real man. He took upon Himself our humanity. "If . . . any praise"—He is the One you can praise and worship today.

You and I live in a dirty world. You cannot walk on the streets of any city without getting dirty. Your mind gets dirty· your eyes get dirty. Do you ever get tired of the filth of it?

Hollywood ran out of ideas years ago, which is the reason Hollywood has dried up. Television is boring; it cannot help but repeat the same old thing. So what have they done? They have substituted filth for genius. Someone has called it the great wasteland. It is like looking at an arid desert, and yet millions keep their eyes glued to it. Their minds are filled with dirt and filth and violence.

If a Christian is going to spend his time with the dirt and filth and questionable things of this world, there will not be power in his life. The reason we have so many weak Christians is that they spend their time with the things of the world, filling their minds and hearts and tummies with the things of this world. Then they wonder why there is no power in their lives.

We need a sanctuary. We need something to think upon that will clean up our minds. Here are some questions to think about: How much time do you spend with the Word of God? How much time do you spend contemplating Christ? "But we all, with open face beholding as in a glass the glory of the Lord, are changed into the same image from glory to glory, even as by the spirit of the Lord" (2 Cor. 3:18). The Word of God is a mirror, and in it we behold the glory of the Lord. The only way you can behold the living Christ is in the Word of God. As you behold Him, there is a liberty, a freedom, and a growth that He gives you. You cannot come by it in any other way.

Oh, how puerile, how inconsequential is the impact of believers' lives! I am amazed at how easily Christians are taken in by every wind of doctrine that comes along. They are not able to discern truth and error. The one explanation, as I have pondered it in my mind, is ignorance of the Word of God. To have power in our lives we must contemplate the person of Jesus Christ, contemplating Him in the Word of God.

Too often people come to the church to be entertained. Someone has said that people come to church to eye the clothes or to close the eyes. Many seem to sit in a daze for an hour just to feel religious or pious. My friend, only the Word of God can bring strength to you. You need physical food when you are weak; you need bread and meat to give you strength. The Word of God is your spiritual bread and meat. The only way to grow spiritually is to spend time in the Word of God. It is the Word that reveals Jesus Christ. I believe He is on every page of Scripture if only we have eyes to see Him. We need to see Him. We need to have the reality of Christ in our lives. This is made possible as we, with an open face, behold the glory of the Lord.

I think one of the things that will cause believers to be ashamed at the appearing of Christ will be their ignorance of the Scriptures when they stand in His presence. I'm of the opinion He will say to many of us, "I gave you all the information you needed in the Scriptures. You didn't listen to Me; you didn't hear Me." We say that one of the problems with our children is that they don't listen to their parents. The problem with the children of God is that they don't listen to their heavenly Father. Contemplation of Christ—that is the sanctuary of power. Many of us need to leave the busyness and dirtiness of this world and go aside with the Wrod of God where we can contemplate Him, worship Him, and praise Him.

**Those things, which ye have both learned, and re-
ceived, and heard, and seen in me, do: and the God of
peace shall be with you [Phil. 4:9].**

A better word for "do" is *practice*. Paul could say something that
would be audacious if you or I said it: "Do what I do." I don't want my
little grandson to follow down the pathway that I went. I don't want
him to have his grandpa for an example. But Paul could make his life
an example to other believers. Paul lived in that sanctuary of power
because He had made Christ the very center and periphery of his life.

IN CHRIST—THE SATISFACTION OF POWER

**But I rejoiced in the Lord greatly, that now at the last
your care of me hath flourished again; wherein ye were
also careful, but ye lacked opportunity [Phil. 4:10].**

At the beginning I said that the Epistle to the Philippians is primar-
ily a thank-you note. Before Paul got down to the thank-you part, he
dealt with Christian experience. He has been talking about Christian
experience throughout the epistle. Now he is thanking them for their
gift.

For two years the church in Philippi had lost touch with Paul.
They did not know where he was after he had been arrested in Jerusalem and then put in prison for two years. The next time they heard
about him, he had been transferred to a prison in Rome. They apolo-
gized to him for not having contact with him and for not communicating their gifts to him during those years. Paul is excusing them in a
most gracious manner. He says, "I rejoiced in the Lord greatly, that
now at the last your care of me hath flourished again; wherein ye were
also careful, but ye lacked opportunity." In other words, "You had lost
contact with me so that you didn't have the opportunity to be helpful
to me." How gracious Paul was!

**Not that I speak in respect of want: for I have learned, in
whatsoever state I am, therewith to be content [Phil.
4:11].**

Paul said that he never made an appeal to them. He never sent out an SOS for help. Paul had learned to be content in whatsoever state he was. It didn't matter whether he was in prison or out of prison. Many of us think that if things are going right and if we are in the right place, then we will be contented. That means that we depend on the circumstances of life for our contentment. I have asked the Lord to give me contentment. I have prayed for Him to make me just as content tape-recording in my office as I am out in Hawaii enjoying the beautiful scenery. Our circumstances have a great deal to do with our contentment, don't they? But Paul had learned to be content regardless of his state.

I know both how to be abased, and I know how to abound: every where and in all things I am instructed both to be full and to be hungry, both to abound and to suffer need [Phil. 4:12].

Paul says, "Though I appreciate your sympathy, I know how to live on the lowest plane economically, and I know how to live on the highest plane. I have done both." There were times when he had nothing, and he was content. There were times when God had given him an abundance, and he had learned how to abound.

When I retired from the pastorate, I told my wife that there would be a terrible letdown in income and in our standard of living. I knew it would be hard for us. Paul knew how to abound and how to be abased, but we're not very good at that. I guess the Lord knew all about it, because due to the generosity of some very wonderful folk our standard hasn't come down. We have been able to live just like we did before. We were prepared to come down, but the Lord didn't bring us down, and we do thank Him and praise His name for it.

It was the custom of Dr. Harry Ironside to go every year to Grand Rapids for a Bible conference at Mel Trotter's mission. Mel Trotter had been an alcoholic, and after he had come to Christ, he opened a mission to reach other men who were in his former condition. The owner of a hotel which had just been built in Grand Rapids had been an alcoholic and had been led to Christ by Mel Trotter. He told Mel, "When

you have a speaker or visitor come to your mission, you send him over
to the hotel. We will keep him here free of charge." When Dr. Ironside
arrived at that hotel, the man ushered him up to the presidential suite.
He had the best apartment in the hotel. Dr. Ironside had never been in
a place like that before. He called Mel on the phone and said, "Listen,
Mel, you don't have to put me up like this. I don't need all this luxury.
All I want is a room with a comfortable bed, and a desk and a lamp
where I can study." Mel assured him that the room was not costing
him or the mission anything; it was being provided free of charge. He
said, "Harry, Paul said he knew how to abound and he knew how to be
abased. Now you learn to abound this week, will you?"

Now we come to a verse that is often quoted, but I think there are
only certain circumstances in which it should be quoted. This verse is
geared to life. It gets down where the rubber meets the road. This
verse needs to be worked out in life.

I can do all things through Christ which strengtheneth me [Phil. 4:13].

This really should be translated the way Paul wrote it: "I can do all
things in Christ which strengtheneth me."

When Paul says *all things*, does he literally mean all things? Does
it mean you can go outside and jump over your house? Of course not.
Paul says, "I can do all things in Christ"—that is, in the context of the
will of Christ for your life. Whatever Christ has for you to do, He will
supply the power. Whatever gift He gives you, He will give the power
to exercise that gift. A gift is a manifestation of the Spirit of God in the
life of the believer. As long as you function in Christ, you will have
power.

Let me give you an illustration. My favorite mode of travel is by
train. I fly only because I must. The train has lots more romance connected with it, and it is much more enjoyable. It gets you there later,
but it gets you there. The Santa Fe Railroad used to have a train called
the Super Chief which ran between Los Angeles and Chicago. That
was a wonderful train, and I enjoyed traveling on it. It traveled with
tremendous power. That Super Chief could say, "I can do all things a

Super Chief is supposed to do on the tracks between Chicago and Los Angeles. I can pull up the Cajon Pass, the highest pass for any railroad in this country. I slow down a little bit, but I do not hesitate. I go right up to the top and down the other side. I can do all things!"

Now suppose the Super Chief had said, "For years I have been taking people back and forth from Chicago to Los Angeles, Los Angeles to Chicago, and it gets a little monotonous. I noticed a little group of people got off at Williams, Arizona, to go to the Grand Canyon. I've been coming by here for years, and I've never seen the Grand Canyon. I think I'll just take off across the desert here and look at the canyon for myself." Now I don't *know* that the train actually ever said that, but I do know that it left the tracks one day over on the side toward the Grand Canyon. I'm here to tell you that it never did make it to the Grand Canyon. The minute it left the tracks, it was a wreck. The train was helpless and hopeless the moment it left the tracks. As long as the Super Chief was on the tracks, as long as it was doing the thing it was supposed to do, it could do all the things a Super Chief should do. It could go up and down over those mountains, back and forth from Chicago to Los Angeles. But it was absolutely helpless when it left the tracks.

This is what Paul is saying about himself—"I can do all things in Christ." Now, friend, if you are a member of Christ's body, He is the Head, and you are to function in the context of His will for your life. His will is the track on which you are to run.

Now Paul is not saying that we can do all things. I can't jump like a grasshopper can jump. When I was in school I was the high jumper, but I can't jump anymore. You see, I can't do *all* things, but I can do all things which God has for me to do from the time He saved me to the time He will take me out of this world.

"Through Christ which strengtheneth me." Christ is the One who will strengthen you and enable you to do all that is in His will for you. He certainly does not mean that He is putting into your hands unlimited power to do anything you want to do. Rather, He will give you the enablement to do all things in the context of His will for you. When you and I are in Christ, and we are moving in Christ on those tracks, we are irresistible. There is no stopping us. But the minute you and I step out of that glorious position, step out of God's will either by sinning, by our own willfulness, or by lack of fellowship, we are as much a wreck as that Santa Fe Super Chief was, and we are not going anywhere. But if we stay on that track, we can do all things in Christ. "If ye abide in me, and my words abide in you, ye shall ask what ye will, and it shall be done unto you" (John 15:7). We had better make sure where we are before we start asking. It is essential to be in His will.

My friend, let me emphasize this: It is essential to be in God's will, and His will is determined by a knowledge of His Bible. So many folk feel that if they can take a little course, it will solve all their problems. Well, it won't solve them. I asked a fellow who paid out quite a sum of money to take a certain course, and he told me how it had helped him and his family—he said it had revolutionized them. Several months later I asked, "How is it going for you now?" He said, "We're just about back where we were before we took the course." Apparently it was not the problem-solver he thought it was. Then I asked him a direct question, "How much time do you really spend in the Word of God?" My friend, the Word of God is the answer; and it's so simple I'm not able to charge for it! Why not forget the little courses that are being offered and get down to a serious study of the Word of God? Don't stop with the Gospel of John, wonderful as it is. There are sixty-five other books in the Bible. If you get the total Word of God, you will get the total will of God for this life, and you will have a basis on which you can operate. There is joy, there is satisfaction and sheer delight in being in the will of God and doing what God wants you to do.

Notwithstanding ye have well done, that ye did communicate with my affliction [Phil. 4:14].

Paul wants them to know that he appreciates their gift—"Ye have done well, that ye did communicate with my affliction." This is his personal thank-you.

Now ye Philippians know also, that in the beginning of the gospel, when I departed from Macedonia, no church communicated with me as concerning giving and receiving, but ye only [Phil. 4:15].

This church was a jewel. There are churches like it across this country today. They have a wonderful fellowship and a heart for the things of God. God is blessing them in marvelous, wonderful ways. The Philippian church was close to the apostle Paul. They were the ones who sent support to him—Paul was their missionary. Wouldn't you have loved to have had Paul as your missionary and to have had a part in his support?

For even in Thessalonica ye sent once and again unto my necessity [Phil. 4:16].

We know from the account in Acts 16 and 17 that Paul had to leave Philippi by the request of the authorities. He went on to Thessalonica where those who opposed the gospel he was preaching set the city in an uproar. No one was helping Paul but the Philippian believers— "For even in Thessalonica ye sent once and again unto my necessity."

Not because I desire a gift: but I desire fruit that may abound to your account [Phil. 4:17].

That church in Philippi has been getting dividends on their contribution right down to the present time. Paul wrote them this epistle to thank them. We are studying the epistle today, and we are profiting from this study. This is a part of the dividends of their contribution. They have stock in the apostle Paul, if you please. They still have a part in getting out the Word of God!

But I have all, and abound: I am full, having received of Epaphroditus the things which were sent from you, an odour of a sweet smell, a sacrifice acceptable, well-pleasing to God [Phil. 4:18].

The priest in the Old Testament went into the holy place to put incense on the altar, and it ascended with a sweet smell. A Christian in his giving is like a priest making an offering to God. When it is made in the right spirit, it is, as Paul is saying to the Philippian believers, more than just making a donation or taking up a collection. It is an offering, an odor of a sweet smell to God. And that is what your gift is when it is given in the right spirit.

> **But my God shall supply all your need according to his riches in glory by Christ Jesus [Phil. 4:19].**

Thinking of their sacrifice to supply his need, Paul assures them that God would supply all their needs. He doesn't say all their *wants*—he doesn't include luxury items—but all their *needs*. However, He does supply luxury items many times. When He does, it is surplus. He does it out of His loving-kindness.

> **Now unto God and our Father be glory for ever and ever. Amen [Phil. 4:20].**

God gets all the glory. He will not share His glory with another.

> **Salute every saint in Christ Jesus. The brethren which are with me greet you.**

> **All the saints salute you, chiefly they that are of Caesar's household [Phil. 4:21–22].**

He greets each believer personally. The believers who are with Paul also send their greetings. Again we are told that some were patricians, nobility, members of the household of Caesar. They now belong to Christ, and they want to be remembered to the Christians in Philippi.

> **The grace of our Lord Jesus Christ be with you all. Amen [Phil. 4:23].**

Paul closes with a benediction, and I will close with a benediction. The grace of our Lord Jesus Christ be with you all. Amen.

BIBLIOGRAPHY
(Recommended for Further Study)

Boice, James Montgomery. *Philippians, an Expository Commentary.* Grand Rapids, Michigan: Zondervan Publishing House, 1971.

Getz, Gene A. *A Profile of Christian Maturity: A Study of Philippians.* Grand Rapids, Michigan: Zondervan Publishing House, 1976.

Gromacki, Robert G. *Stand United in Joy: An Exposition of Philippians.* Grand Rapids, Michigan: Baker Book House, 1980.

Hendriksen, William. *A Commentary on Philippians.* Grand Rapids, Michigan: Baker Book House, 1963.

Ironside, H. A. *Notes on Philippians.* Neptune, New Jersey: Loizeaux Brothers, n.d.

Johnstone, Robert. *Lectures on Philippians.* Grand Rapids, Michigan: Baker Book House, 1875. (An excellent, comprehensive treatment.)

Kelly, William. *Lectures on Philippians and Colossians.* Addison, Illinois: Bible Truth Publishers, n.d.

King, Guy H. *The Joy Way.* Fort Washington, Pennsylvania: Christian Literature Crusade, 1952. (A splendid devotional study in Philippians.)

McGee, J. Vernon. *Probing Through Philippians.* Pasadena, California: Thru the Bible Books, 1971.

Meyer, F. B. *The Epistle to the Philippians.* Grand Rapids, Michigan: Kregel Publications. (Devotional.)

Moule, Handley C. G. *Studies in Philippians.* Grand Rapids, Michigan: Kregel Publications, 1893. (This is a reprint from *The Cambridge University Bible for Schools and Colleges* and covers Romans, Ephesians, Philippians, and Colossians. Very helpful.)

Muller, Jac J. *The Epistle of Paul to the Philippians and to Philemon.* Grand Rapids, Michigan: Wm. B. Eerdmans Publishing Co., 1955.

Pentecost, J. Dwight. *The Joy of Living.* Grand Rapids, Michigan: Zondervan Publishing House, 1973. (A practical study of Philippians.)

Robertson, A. T. *Epochs in the Life of Paul.* Grand Rapids, Michigan: Baker Book House, 1909.

Robertson, A. T. *Paul's Joy in Christ: Studies in Philippians.* Grand Rapids, Michigan: Baker Book House, 1917. (Excellent.)

Strauss, Lehman. *Devotional Studies in Philippians.* Neptune, New Jersey: Loizeaux Brothers, 1959.

Vine, W. E. *Philippians and Colossians.* London: Oliphants, 1955. (Excellent treatment by a Greek scholar.)

Vos, Howard. *Philippians—A Study Guide.* Grand Rapids, Michigan: Zondervan Publishing House, 1975. (Excellent for individual or group study.)

Walvoord, John F. *Philippians: Triumph in Christ.* Chicago, Illinois: Moody Press, 1971. (Excellent, inexpensive survey.)

Wiersbe, Warren W. *Be Joyful.* Wheaton, Illinois: Victor Books, n.d.

Wuest, Kenneth S. *Philippians in the Greek New Testament.* Grand Rapids, Michigan: Wm. B. Eerdmans Publishing Co., 1942.

COLOSSIANS

The Epistle to the

COLOSSIANS

INTRODUCTION

The author of this epistle is the apostle Paul as stated in Colossians 1:1.

The Epistle to the Colossians is one of the Prison Epistles which are so called because they were written by Paul while he was in prison in Rome. The Prison Epistles include Ephesians, Philippians, Colossians, and the very personal Epistle to Philemon.

The year was about A.D. 62. Four messengers left Rome unobserved, but they each carried a very valuable document. Tychicus was carrying the Epistle to the Ephesians over to Ephesus where he was the pastor or the leader of that church. Epaphroditus was carrying the Epistle to the Philippians as he was the pastor in Philippi. Epaphras was carrying the Epistle to the Colossians; apparently he was the leader of the church in Colosse. Onesimus was carrying the Epistle to Philemon. Philemon was his master, and Onesimus, who had run away, was returning to him.

These four are companion epistles and together have been called the anatomy of Christianity, or the anatomy of the church. We can see that the subjects of these epistles cover all aspects of the Christian faith:

Ephesians is about the body of believers called the church, of which Christ is the head.

Colossians directs our attention to the head of the body who is Christ. The body itself is secondary. Christ is the theme. He is the center of the circle around which all Christian living revolves. Colossians emphasizes the plērōma; Christ is the fullness of God.

Philippians shows the church walking here on earth. Christian living is the theme; it is the periphery of the circle of which Christ is the center. Philippians emphasizes the *kenōsis*, Christ becoming a servant.

Philemon gives us Christianity in action. We would say it is where the rubber meets the road, or in that day it was where the sandals touched the Roman road. It demonstrates Christianity worked out in a pagan society.

We can see why these four documents have been called the anatomy of the church—they belong together to make a whole.

I don't think any armored car ever carried four more valuable documents. Do you realize that if today you possessed those four original documents as they came from the hand of Paul, you could probably get any price you wanted for them—you would have the wealth of a king! Well, we measure it in terms other than the dollar sign; their spiritual value cannot be estimated in human terms at all.

I have never been to Colosse although I have been in sight of it—I have seen it from a distance. The ruins of it stand there in the gates of Phrygia. It is over in the same area where Laodicea and Hierapolis are. There are some ruins of the city; there are no ruins of any church. The church at Colosse met in the home of Philemon. I doubt that there ever was a church building there.

A great civilization and a great population were in that area. It was more or less a door to the Orient, to the East; it was called the gates of Phrygia. Here the East and the West met. Here is where the Roman Empire attempted to tame the East and to bring it under Roman subjugation.

Colosse was a great fortress city as were Laodicea, Philadelphia, Sardis, Thyatira, and Pergamum. All of these had been great cities of defense against invasion from the East. But by the time of Paul the apostle the danger had been relieved because the Roman Empire was pretty much in charge of the world by then. As a result, the people had lapsed into paganism and gross immorality at the time of Paul. And Colosse was typical of the great cities of that day.

As far as the record is concerned, Paul never visited the city of Colosse. After I visited the Bible lands I could understand many things in Scripture that I had not understood before. Why didn't Paul visit Colosse? It seems that he did not come in through the gates of Phrygia, but instead he came into the north of Colosse over at Sardis. Apparently he took that Roman road to Ephesus and by-passed Colosse.

Even though Paul was never in the city of Colosse, he was the founder of the church there. Epaphras was the leader of the church, and he may have been the *direct* founder, but Paul founded the church at Colosse. He was the founder in very much the same way as he was the founder of the church at Rome: he touched multitudes of people in the Roman Empire who later gravitated to Rome and formed the church there. Paul may have visited Laodicea (although I doubt that very seriously), and believers may have come from there to Colosse. But converts from Paul's ministry in Ephesus very definitely could have come to Colosse to form the nucleus of that church. Colosse is located just seventy-five to one hundred miles east of Ephesus.

Paul spent three years of ministry in Ephesus, two of them teaching in the school of Tyrannus. There was a tremendous civilization in that area—the culture of the Roman Empire was centered there. It was no longer centered in Greece, which had pretty much deteriorated along with her philosophy and culture. But the Greek culture was virile in Asia Minor, the area known as Turkey today. It was in this area that Paul did his greatest work along with his co-workers. There were with him John Mark, Barnabas, Silas, Timothy, and apparently some of the other apostles. We know that the apostle John became the pastor at Ephesus later on.

Asia Minor was a great cultural center, but it was also a center for heathenism, paganism, and the mystery religions. There was already abroad that which is known as Gnosticism, the first heresy of the church. There were many forms of Gnosticism, and in Colosse there were the Essenes. There are three points of identification for this group:

1. They had an *exclusive spirit.* They were the aristocrats in wisdom. They felt that they were the people—they had knowledge in a jug and held the stopper in their hands. They felt they had the monopoly of it all. As a result, they considered themselves super-duper in

knowledge and thought they knew more than any of the apostles. Paul will issue them a warning in the first chapter: "Whom we preach, warning every man, and teaching every man in all wisdom; that we may present every man perfect in Christ Jesus" (Col. 1:28). Perfection is not to be found in any cult or any heresy, but in Christ Jesus. All wisdom is found in Him.

2. They held *speculative tenets on creation*. They taught that God did not create the universe directly, but created a creature who in turn created another creature, until one finally created the physical universe. Christ was considered a creature in this long series of creations. This was known in pantheistic Greek philosophy as the *demiurge*. Paul refutes this in Colossians 1:15–19 and 2:18.

3. Another identifying mark of this group was their ethical practice of *asceticism and unrestrained licentiousness*. They got the asceticism from the influence of Greek Stoicism and the unrestrained licentiousness from the influence of Greek Epicureanism. Paul refutes this in Colossians 2:16, 23 and 3:5–9.

Colossians is the chart and compass which enables the believer to sail between the ever present Scylla and Charybdis. On the one hand there is always the danger of Christianity freezing into a form, into a ritual. It has done that in many areas and in many churches so that Christianity involves nothing more than going through a routine. On the other hand is the danger that Christianity will evaporate into a philosophy. I had an example of that when a man who was liberal in his theology asked me, "What theory of inspiration do you hold?" I answered him, "I don't hold a *theory* of inspiration. I believe that the Word of God is the revelation of God as it says it is. That is not a theory." We find people talking about theories of inspiration and theories of atonement—that is the evaporation of Christianity into a philosophy.

So there are two dangers. One is to freeze into form and become nothing but a ritualistic church; the other is to evaporate into steam and be lost in liberalism and false philosophy. You will remember that the Lord Jesus said that He was the Water of Life. He didn't say, "I am the ice of life"; neither did he say, "I am the steam of life." He is the

Water of Life—water at the temperature of life, neither freezing nor boiling.

The Water of Life is "Christ in you, the hope of glory" (Col. 1:27). Christ is to live in you. He is to walk down the street where you live. Christianity is Christ down where we live, Christ in the nitty-gritty of life, down where the rubber meets the road.

There has always been the danger of adding something to or subtracting something from Christ—the oldest heresy is also the newest heresy, by the way. Christianity is not a mathematical problem of adding or subtracting: Christianity is Christ. This is what Paul teaches in this epistle: "For in him dwelleth all the fulness of the Godhead bodily" (Col. 2:9)—in Him dwelleth all the plērōma. All you need is to be found in Christ Jesus.

Here is a quotation from William Sanday: "In the Ephesian Epistle the church is the primary object, and the thought passes upward to Christ as the head of the church. In the Colossian Epistle Christ is the primary object, and the thought passes downward to the church as the body of Christ."

The dominating thought in this epistle is: Christ is all. He is all I need; He is everything. Charles Wesley put it like this in his lovely hymn: "Thou, O Christ, art all I want; more than all in Thee I find."

Charles Spurgeon said, "Look on thine own nothingness; be humble, but look at Jesus, thy great representative, and be glad. It will save thee many pangs if thou will learn to think of thyself as being *in Him*"—accepted in the Beloved, finding Him our all in all.

I received a letter from a dear lady here in Pasadena. She is eighty years old and doesn't expect to live much longer, but she is resting in Christ's loving forgiveness. My friend, you cannot find a better place to rest.

If you are resting in Him, you will find that you don't need to go through a ritual. You won't need to do a lot of gyrations and genuflections. You won't be discussing the theories of inspiration. You either believe that the Bible is the Word of God, or you don't believe it is the Word of God.

Let us stop this so-called intellectual approach that we find in our churches today. It's no good. When I started out as a pastor, I tried to be intellectual. An elder in the church in which I served came to me and talked to me about it, and he said, "We would rather have a genuine Vernon McGee than an imitation of anybody else." You see, I was trying to imitate intellectual men whom I admired. We don't need to do that kind of thing—we need to be ourselves. We need to get down off our high horses. Remember that the Lord Jesus is feeding sheep, not giraffes.

The practical section of this epistle shows us Christ, the fullness of God, poured out in the lives of the believers. The alabaster box of ointment needs to be broken today. The world not only needs to see something, but it needs to smell something. The pollution of this world is giving a very bad odor in these days. We need something of the fragrance and loveliness of Jesus Christ, and only the church is permitted to break that alabaster box of ointment and let out the fragrance.

OUTLINE

I. **Doctrinal: Christ, the Fullness *(plērōma)* of God; in Christ We Are Made Full, Chapters 1—2**
   A. Introduction, Chapter 1:1–8
   B. Paul's Prayer, Chapter 1:9–14
   C. Person of Christ, Chapter 1:15–19
   D. Objective Work of Christ for Sinners, Chapter 1:20–23
   E. Subjective Work of Christ for Saints, Chapter 1:24–29
   F. Christ, the Answer to Philosophy (For the Head), Chapter 2:1–15
   G. Christ, the Answer to Ritual (For the Heart), Chapter 2:16–23

II. **Practical: Christ, the Fullness of God, Poured Out in Life through Believers, Chapters 3—4**
   A. Thoughts and Affections of Believers Are Heavenly, Chapter 3:1–4
   B. Living of Believers Is Holy, Chapters 3:5—4:6
   C. Fellowship of Believers Is Hearty, Chapter 4:7–18

CHAPTER 1

THEME: Christ, the fullness of God—in Christ we are
made full; Introduction; Paul's prayer; person of
Christ; objective work of Christ for sinners; subjective
work of Christ for saints

INTRODUCTION

The four Prison Epistles of Paul, which include the Epistle to the
Colossians, have been called the anatomy of the Church because
their subjects cover all aspects of the Christian faith. In Colossians our
attention is directed to the head of the body who is Christ. The body,
the church, is secondary. Instead, Christ is the theme, and Christian
living is centered in Him.

> **Paul, an apostle of Jesus Christ by the will of God, and
> Timotheus our brother,**
>
> **To the saints and faithful brethren in Christ which are
> at Colosse: Grace be unto you, and peace, from God our
> Father and the Lord Jesus Christ [Col. 1:1–2].**

Paul calls himself "an apostle of Jesus Christ," and he always says it is
"by the will of God." Paul was in the will of God when he was an
apostle. *God* made him an apostle.

Are you in the will of God today? Are you serving Christ? Are you
sure you are in the proper place? Are you sure you are doing the
proper thing? I believe that every believer is called to *function* in the
body of believers, but it is important to be functioning in the right
way. There are too many people who are active, doing something that
they are not supposed to be doing. Too often we try to imitate other
people. We think, "I'll get busy doing what brother so-and-so is doing." We need to remember that our gifts are different, and we are each
going to function a little differently. But we ought to be *functioning.*
God made Paul an apostle. Did God put you where you are? When you

know you are in the will of God, there is a deep satisfaction in life, by the way.

"To the saints and faithful brethren in Christ which are at Colosse." He is not talking about two groups of people. The saints and the believing brethren are the same. Faithful brethren are believing brethren, and they are saints. We are not saints because of what we do. We are saints by our position. The Greek word for *saints* means "to be set apart for God." Those who are set apart for God and the believing brethren are the same group of people.

Notice that they are "in Christ" but they are "at Colosse." The most important question is not, Where are you *at?* but Who are you *in?* That may not be good grammar, but it sure is good Bible. The saints are *at Colosse*—it is important that we have an address down here. But we ought to have an address up yonder also: *in Christ.*

"Grace be unto you, and peace, from God our Father and the Lord Jesus Christ." We must know the grace of God in order to experience the peace of God.

In the better manuscripts "and the Lord Jesus Christ" is not added. It says simply, "Grace be unto you, and peace, from God our Father." It is important to remember that Paul is writing to counteract Gnosticism, which was the first heresy in the church. This was the Essene branch of Gnosticism. They relegated God to a place far removed from man and taught that one had to go through emanations to get to God. Have you ever noticed that all heathen religions and cults have some sort of an "open sesame" before you can get in to God? Paul makes it very clear here that grace and peace come directly "from God our Father." We can come directly to Him through Christ.

We give thanks to God and the Father of our Lord Jesus Christ, praying always for you [Col. 1:3].

We can go *directly* to God. We do not need to go through any form of emanation at all. Anyone who is in Christ Jesus has access to God the Father. One of the benefits of being justified by faith is access to God through our Lord Jesus Christ.

"Praying always for you." You would find it very challenging to compile a list of the folk Paul said he was praying for, and add the Colossian believers to the list. He always prayed for them; they were on his prayer list.

Since we heard of your faith in Christ Jesus, and of the love which ye have to all the saints,

For the hope which is laid up for you in heaven, whereof ye heard before in the word of the truth of the gospel [Col. 1:4–5].

Here Paul links the trinity of graces for believers: (1) faith—past; (2) love—present; and (3) hope—future.

Paul is going to talk about the good points of these believers. They had *faith* toward God. Faith rests upon historical facts; it is based on the past. It was based on what they had heard before "in the word of the truth of the gospel." This refers to the content of the gospel, the great truths that pertain to the gospel of the grace of God. God has us shut up to a cross, and He asks us to believe Him. You haven't really heard the gospel until you have heard something to believe. The gospel is not something for us to do. It tells what *He* did for you and for me over nineteen hundred years ago. "So then faith cometh by hearing, and hearing by the word of God" (Rom. 10:17). Faith is not a leap in the dark. It rests upon historical facts; it is believing God.

"And of the love which ye have to all the saints"—faith is based upon the past, but *love* is for the present.

It is nonsense today to boast of the fundamentalism of our doctrine and then to spend our time crucifying our brethren and attempting to find fault with them. There are too many "wonderful saints" looking down on their fellow believers who have not measured up to their high standard and who are not separated like they are separated. My friend, the world is not interested in that kind of approach. The world is looking to see whether Christians love each other or not. It is hypocrisy to consider oneself a Christian and then not to demonstrate love for the brethren. If we have disagreements with our brethren, we are to bear with them, we are to pray for them, and we are to love them.

Remember that a Christian is a sinner saved by grace. None of us will ever be perfect in this life.

A man came to me to criticize a certain Christian leader—and I don't agree with everything that leader does either—but the Spirit of God is using that man in a mighty way. So I asked the man who was complaining, "Do you ever pray for him?" He answered, "No, I don't." I replied, "I think that you ought to pray for him. You may not agree with him on every point, but the Spirit of God is using him."

These Colossian believers had their good points. They were sound in the faith toward God. They were fundamental in their belief, and they also had love for the brethren. And Paul says that they had hope for the future—"For the hope which is laid up for you in heaven."

In 1 Corinthians also Paul lists these three graces, but he lists them a little differently: "And now abideth faith, hope, charity, these three; but the greatest of these is charity" (1 Cor. 13:13). He puts hope in second position and love is listed last. Why? Because love is the only thing that is going to abide. Love is for the present, it is true, but it is also going to make it into eternity. It is very important that we begin to exhibit love down here upon this earth, don't you agree?

That "hope which is laid up for you in heaven" is the blessed hope. We are to look for the coming of Christ; we are to love His appearing.

"Whereof ye heard before in the word of the truth [content] of the gospel." The gospel is a simple message which God simply asks you to believe. You are asked to believe on the basis of certain facts: Jesus Christ was virgin born. He performed miracles. He is the God-man. He died on a cross, was buried, and rose again. He ascended back into heaven. He sent the Holy Spirit into the world on the Day of Pentecost to form the church. And He is sitting at God's right hand today; His position there indicates that our redemption is complete. We are asked to enter into the rest which He offers to those who will come to Him. He has a present ministry of intercession for us. I think He has other ministries, too. And finally, He is going to return to this earth again. These are all part of the glorious gospel. This is the "content" of the gospel, as Paul expresses it here.

Which is come unto you, as it is in all the world; and bringeth forth fruit, as it doth also in you, since the day ye heard of it, and knew the grace of God in truth [Col. 1:6].

Paul says the gospel has come to the Colossians as it has come to "all the world." Dr. Marvin R. Vincent, a great expositor of the Epistle to the Colossians, as well as other expositors, believes this is hyperbole. I'll be honest with you, I also had difficulty accepting this statement. Is Paul trying to say that at this particular time when he was in prison in Rome the gospel had reached the world? That is what he says. I have come to the position that I believe he meant what he said *literally;* it is not hyperbole. When I visited Asia Minor, I stood in Turkey at the city of Sardis and saw part of a Roman road that had been uncovered by excavation. That is the road that Paul traveled when he came down out of the Galatian country on the way to Ephesus. For three years he preached the gospel in Ephesus to people who were there from all over the Roman Empire. As a result, the gospel had gone ahead to Rome long before Paul was taken there as a prisoner.

The word for "world" here is *kosmos,* and it simply means the Roman Empire of that day. The gospel at that time had penetrated into the farthest reaches of the Roman Empire. It may have even crossed over to Great Britain. Every part of the Roman world had heard the gospel. I tell you, my friend, those early apostles were on the move! I am reluctant to criticize anything they did. Paul says here that the gospel had gone into all the Roman world.

"And bringeth forth fruit." Wherever the gospel is preached it will bring forth fruit. Paul says that, and it is true.

I must confess my faith was weak when we began our radio program. I determined to give out the Word of God, but I'll be honest with you, I expected to fall on my face and see great failure. The biggest surprise of my life was that God blessed His Word. Was I surprised! I thought He would let me down, but He didn't. He said He would bless His Word, and we can count on Him to do that. It "bringeth forth fruit, as it doth also in you, since the day ye heard of it, and knew the grace of God in truth." I am overwhelmed today by the letters and by the people I meet who say they were brought to Christ through our radio ministry. It started out so weakly. It was just a Mickey Mouse operation if there ever was one. But God blesses His Word. I don't only believe that; I know it. I won't even argue with anybody about that. Some fellow comes to me and says, "Dr. McGee, I don't believe the Bible is the Word of God." And I say, "You don't?" He says, "No. Aren't you going to argue with me to persuade me?" I say, "Well, no." And he asks, "Why not?" I have to say, "Because I know it is the Word of God. I don't only believe it; I know it."

It would be just as if someone came to me and said, "Dr. McGee, I want to argue with you about whether you love your wife or not. I can give you several philosophical arguments that will show that you don't love your wife." Do you know, that fellow might out-argue me and whip me down intellectually. He might show me by logic and all types of argument that I don't love my wife. Do you know what I would say? I'd say, "Brother, I don't know about those arguments, but I want you to know one thing: I love my wife." You see, that is something I know. I know I love her. I don't need all those cogent, sophisticated, astute, esoteric arguments. There are some things we simply know.

And we should not let what we don't know upset what we do know. That is important for us to see. Paul says that the gospel *will* bring forth fruit. That is the wonderful confidence that we can have.

As ye also learned of Epaphras our dear fellow-servant, who is for you a faithful minister of Christ [Col. 1:7].

Apparently Epaphras was the leader or the pastor of the church in Colosse. (*Epaphras* sounds like the name of a medicine to me, but nevertheless, that was the name of the fellow.) Paul calls him "our dear fellow-servant." Have you noticed how graciously Paul could talk about other servants of God? Paul had something good to say about those who were preaching the Word of God. But when he found a rascal, he was just like our Lord in that he would really reprimand evil when he saw it.

The Lord Jesus was so merciful to sinners. The woman taken in adultery should have been stoned to death, but notice how gracious our Lord was to her (see John 8:1–11). Then there was that arrogant Pharisee, Nicodemus, who came to the Lord Jesus and attempted to pay Him a compliment: ". . . Rabbi, we know that thou art a teacher come from God" (John 3:2). In effect, "We Pharisees know. And, brother, when we know something, that's it!" The Lord Jesus so gently and so graciously pulled him down off his high horse. When the Lord got through with him, he was just plain, little old Nicky. Little old Nicodemus was trying to be somebody, but he was nothing in the world but a religious robot going through rituals. The Lord Jesus brought him down to the place where he could humbly ask, "How can these things be?" Then the Lord Jesus led him to see the Cross. How gracious He was in dealing with folk like that!

Who also declared unto us your love in the Spirit [Col. 1:8].

We will not find a great emphasis on the Holy Spirit in this epistle, but Paul does make it clear to the Colossian believers that they would not have been able to exhibit this love unless it were by the Holy Spirit. It was to the Galatians that Paul wrote that the fruit of the Spirit is love. In this epistle he will not dwell on that aspect. He is going to dwell on the person of Christ. As he does that, the Spirit of God will take the things of Christ and will show them unto us. That is the important work of the Holy Spirit.

PAUL'S PRAYER

In this next section we have Paul's prayer for the Colossians. This is one of the most wonderful prayers in Scripture. It is a prayer that I think touches all the bases, and it will be very helpful for us to notice what Paul prays for.

It is very interesting that today we find people who are praying *for* these things. Paul makes it clear that we already *have* these things. Dr. H. A. Ironside speaks of the prayers that we hear people say which go something like this: "We pray Thee, forgive us our sins and wash us in the blood of Jesus. Receive us into Thy kingdom. Give us of Thy Holy Spirit, and save us at last for Christ's sake. Amen." Did you know that God has already answered every one of those petitions? God has forgiven us all our trespasses. We are cleansed by the blood of Christ. He has already translated us out of the kingdom of darkness into the kingdom of the Son of His love. He has sealed us with His Holy Spirit. ". . . if any man have not the Spirit of Christ, he is none of his" (Rom. 8:9). He has saved us eternally from the very moment we first believed the gospel. Therefore it would be more fitting to thank and praise Him for all these things than to be petitioning Him for what we already have. Instead of praying, "We ask this of Thee," the prayer should be, "We thank Thee for all that You have already done."

Now we come to this wonderful prayer that Paul prayed. First he will make several petitions, and then he will thank the Lord for the things He has already done for us.

> **For this cause we also, since the day we heard it, do not cease to pray for you, and to desire that ye might be filled with the knowledge of his will in all wisdom and spiritual understanding [Col. 1:9].**

The first thing for which Paul prayed was that they might be filled with knowledge. The Greek word is *epignōsis* which means "a super knowledge." The Gnostics, the heretics there in Colosse, boasted that they had a super knowledge. Paul says here, "I pray that you might be filled with knowledge, that you might have a super knowledge." But Paul confines this knowledge to knowledge of the will of God—this knowledge must be "in all wisdom and spiritual understanding."

Let me merely call attention to the fact that the word *wisdom* occurs six times in this short epistle.

> **That ye might walk worthy of the Lord unto all pleasing, being fruitful in every good work, and increasing in the knowledge of God [Col. 1:10].**

His second petition is that they might be pleasing to God. That means that these Christians will not be bowing down to men or attempting to please them.

His third request is that they might be "fruitful in every good work." The Christian is a fruit-bearing branch. Christ is the vine, and we should bring forth fruit.

"Increasing in the knowledge of God." A Christian should not be static but alive and growing in the Word of God. So their increase in the knoweldge of God is Paul's fourth request.

Strengthened with all might, according to his glorious power, unto all patience and longsuffering with joyfulness [Col. 1:11].

Here is his fifth request. Strength and power can come only from God; they are produced by the Holy Spirit. These believers are to be strengthened with all might "unto all patience and longsuffering." And this patience and longsuffering is to be "with joyfulness."

Giving thanks unto the Father, which hath made us meet to be partakers of the inheritance of the saints in light [Col. 1:12].

Here is the beginning of the list of things for which Paul is thankful. All our prayers should be filled with thanksgiving. Paul is thankful that God by His grace has given us an inheritance with the saints in light. We ought to lay hold of that today. We should believe God and believe that His promise is true.

Who hath delivered us from the power of darkness, and hath translated us into the kingdom of his dear Son [Col. 1:13].

Paul is thankful that we have been delivered from the kingdom of Satan. We were dead in trespasses and sins, going the way of the world.

Now we have been translated into the kingdom of the Son of His love. This is the present aspect of the kingdom of God here on earth today. You can't build the kingdom of God. The only way you can be a part of it is to open your heart and receive Christ as your Savior. That translates you into the kingdom of His dear Son.

In whom we have redemption through his blood, even the forgiveness of sins [Col. 1:14].

Not only have we been translated into His kingdom, but we also have forgiveness of sins in Him. This is always associated with the blood of Christ. God does not arbitrarily and sentimentally forgive sins. We have redemption through His blood—"redemption" is *apolutrōsis* which means "to set free an enslaved people." He paid a price to deliver us out of slavery.

Paul has given thanks for five wonderful truths. If we are trusting Christ, God has made us meet to be partakers of the inheritance of the saints in light. He has delivered us from the power of darkness and has translated us into the kingdom of His dear Son. God has redeemed us through Christ and has forgiven us our sins through His blood. Yet there are a great many Christian people today who pray for all five of these things. My believing friend, they are yours. Why don't you thank Him for them?

PERSON OF CHRIST

We spoke of the person of Jesus Christ in our study of the Song of Solomon. In Colossians we come in close on the subject and learn the theology of it. This is a very lofty, very exalted, and very grand section of this epistle. The subject here is the person of Jesus Christ. We cannot say too much about Him, and we will never in this life be able to comprehend Him in all of His wonder and in all of His glory.

This section provides an answer to those who would deny the deity of Jesus Christ. To understand these verses is to realize how wonderful He really is. Paul is specifically attempting to answer one of the oldest heresies in the church, Gnosticism. Another of the first heresies was Arianism. Arius of Alexandria said that the Lord Jesus Christ was a creature, a created being. The Council of Nicaea in A.D. 325 answered this heresy saying, "The Son is very Man of very man, and very God of very God." Later on in the history of the church, Socinus propagated the heresy that Jesus was not God and that mankind did not need a Savior from sin. He taught that we were not totally depraved. Today this is the basis of Unitarianism and some of the cults, including Jehovah's Witnesses.

There are given here nine marks of identification of Christ which make Him different from and superior to any other person who has ever lived.

Who is the image of the invisible God, the firstborn of every creature [Col. 1:15].

1. He is the "image of the invisible God." "Image" is eikōn. How could He be the image of the invisible God? You cannot take a photograph or an image of that which is invisible. How could He be that? John makes this clear in the prologue to his gospel: "In the beginning was the Word." That is a beginning that has no beginning—Christ has no beginning. "In the beginning was the Word, and the Word was with God, and the Word was God" (John 1:1). And then John says, "And the Word was made [born] flesh . . ." (John 1:14). If you want the Christmas story in John's gospel, that is it: He was born flesh. This is the way that He became the image of the invisible God. How could He be that? Because He is God. If He were not God, He could not have been the image of the invisible God.

2. He is "the firstborn of every creature." This reveals His relationship to the Father and His position in the Trinity. God is the everlasting Father; the Son is the everlasting Son. His position in the Trinity is that of Son.

"Firstborn" indicates His priority before all creation. His headship of all creation does not mean that He was born first. We need to understand what the Scriptures mean by "firstborn."

Nowhere does Scripture teach that Jesus Christ had His beginning at Bethlehem. We are told in the great prophecy of Micah 5:2 that He would be born in Bethlehem, but that He came forth from everlasting. Isaiah 9:6 tells us, "For unto us a child is born, unto us a son is given. . . ." The child is born, but the Son is given. He came out of eternity and took upon Himself our humanity.

Paul is dealing with one of the philosophies of that day, one of the mystery religions. It is called the demiurge, and it held that God created a creature just beneath Him; then that creature created a creature beneath him; then that creature created a creature beneath him. You can just keep on going down that ladder until finally you come to a creature that created this universe. These were emanations from God. Gnosticism taught that Jesus was one of these creatures, an emanation from God. Now Paul is answering that. He says that Jesus Christ is the Firstborn of all creation, He is back of all creation. The Greek word is prōtotokos meaning "before all creation." He was not born in creation. He is the One who came down over nineteen hundred years ago and became flesh. He existed before any creation: "In the beginning was the Word, and the Word was with God, and the Word was God. The same was in the beginning with God. All things were made by him; and without him was not any thing made that was made" (John 1:1–3). God the Father is the everlasting Father. God the Son is the everlasting Son. There never was a time when Christ was begotten.

There are several places in Scripture where the Lord Jesus is called the Firstborn. He is called the Firstborn of all creation; He is called the Firstborn from the dead; and He is called the only begotten.

He is called the Firstborn from the dead later in this first chapter, verse 18. This is what the psalmist spoke of: "I will declare the decree: the LORD hath said unto me, Thou art my Son; this day have I begotten thee" (Ps. 2:7). Paul explained this idea further in that great sermon that he preached at Antioch of Pisidia in the Galatian country. Paul said there that the psalmist meant that Christ was begotten from the dead: "And we declare unto you glad tidings, how that the promise which was made unto the fathers, God hath fulfilled the same unto us their children, in that he hath raised up Jesus again; as it is also written in the second psalm, Thou art my Son, this day have I begotten thee" (Acts 13:32–33).

When Jesus Christ is called the Firstborn of all creation, it is not referring to His birth at Bethlehem. This is no Christmas verse. It means that He has top priority of position. It has nothing to do with His origin at all. The psalmist wrote, "Also I will make him my first-born, higher than the kings of the earth" (Ps. 89:27). This makes it very clear that Christ as the eternal Son holds the position of top priority to all creation. In other words, He is the Creator. There is no demi-urge, no series of creatures being created one after another. He Himself created all things.

Let me mention some other verses of Scripture that speak of the person of Christ. In Hebrews 1:3 we read: "Who being the brightness of his glory, and the express image of his person, and upholding all things by the word of his power, when he had by himself purged our sins, sat down on the right hand of the Majesty on high." That doesn't sound very much like He is a mere creature, does it? He is the Second Person of the Godhead. "And of the angels he saith, Who maketh his angels spirits, and his ministers a flame of fire." Now the Lord Jesus is not one of these creatures: "But unto the Son he saith, Thy throne, O God, is for ever and ever: a sceptre of righteousness is the sceptre of thy kingdom" (Heb. 1:7–8).

So, my friend, what we are talking about here is not that the Lord Jesus was born a creature; we are talking about the fact that He is God. When He came into the world, a child was born but *the Son was given*, and He had come out of eternity. The angel's announcement to Mary was ". . . that holy thing which shall be born of thee shall be called the Son of God" (Luke 1:35). Why? Because that is who He is. He was the Son of God before He came into this world. ". . . Thou art the Christ, the Son of the living God" (Matt. 16:16).

Now we come to the next two great statements concerning the Lord Jesus:

> **For by him were all things created, that are in heaven, and that are in earth, visible and invisible, whether they be thrones, or dominions, or principalities, or powers: all things were created by him, and for him [Col. 1:16].**

3. "By him were all things created." If all things were created by Him, that clears up the question of His being a creature or the Creator. The statement that He is the Firstborn of all creation does not mean that He was created, but rather He is the One who did the creating.

There are two kinds of creation, the "visible and invisible." It is very interesting here to note that he mentions different gradations of rank in spiritual intelligences: thrones, dominions, principalities, powers. There are gradations in the angelic hosts. Other verses in Scripture tell us that there are seraphim and cherubim, and also the archangels. And then there are just the common, everyday, vegetable variety of angels.

In Ephesians we note the fact that our enemy is a spiritual enemy. Satan has a spiritual host that rebelled with him. So there are different gradations of rank among our spiritual enemies, too.

4. It is wonderful to know that all things were created by Him. But there is another truth given to us here: All things were created "for him."

If you were to go out tonight and look up at the heavens, you would see a number of stars. Have you ever wondered why each star is in its own special position? Why is that star in that part of the heavens? It is in that part of the heavens because that is where Jesus wanted it. Not only did He create all things, but they were created *for* Him.

One of the most wonderful truths in this connection is that we are told that we are heirs of God and joint-heirs with the Lord Jesus Christ. We have a big hunk of real estate coming to us someday. Maybe He will turn over a whole star to us. I don't know; I have often wondered. I think we will be very busy in eternity. We will not be earthlings then, but we will be given a new body which is free from gravitation. We will be living in a city called the New Jerusalem. We will be able to travel through God's vast universe. I don't know how much of that universe He is going to turn over to us. He made it all, created it out of nothing, and He is going to run it to suit Himself. This is *His* universe. If you have wondered why a certain tree has a certain kind of leaf, it is because that is the way He wanted it. It was made *by* Him, and it was made *for* Him. We are going to enter into that someday: there is an inheritance prepared for us. I have never dwelt upon that very much because I feel that it is rather speculative. But I am sure that all of us wonder what it will be like when we are with Him in eternity. We do know it will be wonderful.

You and I are living down here in tents. Paul calls these bodies of ours just that—tents. He says, "For we know that if our earthly house of this tabernacle were dissolved . . ." (2 Cor. 5:1). A tabernacle is a tent. This tent will go right back to the ground because the body is to be put into the ground at death. We will have moved out of our tent. He says, ". . . willing rather to be absent from the body, and to be present with the Lord" (2 Cor. 5:8). When we are absent from these old bodies down here, we will be present with the Lord. We will be at home with Him.

You may be living in a home that cost $500,000. I have news for you: you are actually living in a flabby, old, frail tent—all of us are. But one of these days we will have our glorified bodies, and then we will receive our inheritance! You can have your $500,000 house—you won't be in it long, anyway. Our new body is for eternity, and we will be at home with Him forever. This is the prospect ahead for the child of God. I'm rather looking forward to it. "All things were created by him, and for him."

And he is before all things, and by him all things consist [Col. 1:17].

5. "He is before all things." All fullness dwells in the preincarnate Christ, and all fullness dwells in the incarnate Christ. "For in him dwelleth all the fulness of the Godhead bodily" (Col. 2:9). We are made complete in Him. He was before all things. He is the preincarnate Christ.

6. "By him all things consist." He holds everything together. He maintains creation. He directs it. "Consist" is *sunistēmi* which means to hold together. He is the super glue of the universe.

A few years ago in our lifetime, man did a very daring, and I think now, a very dastardly deed: he untied the atom. The Lord Jesus tied each one of those little fellows together when He created the atom. Man did what he called splitting the atom. Believe me, did he release power! Have you ever stopped to think of the tremendous power that there is in the atoms of this universe? If one bomb that we can hold in our hand can blow a whole area to smithereens, then how much power is tied up on this vast physical universe? Who is holding all that together? We are told that Christ not only created it but that He holds it together. I would say that holding it all together is a pretty big job. The Lord Jesus Christ is the One who is able to do that.

We have this same truth repeated for us in Hebrews: "Who being the brightness of his glory, and the express image of his person, and upholding all things by the word of his power, when he had by himself purged our sins, sat down on the right hand of the Majesty on high" (Heb. 1:3). He's a wonderful person, isn't He? He's a glorious person!

> **And he is the head of the body, the church: who is the beginning, the firstborn from the dead; that in all things he might have the preeminence [Col. 1:18].**

7. "He is the head of the body, the church." I believe this is the key to the Epistle to the Colossians, which is really a companion epistle to the Epistles to the Ephesians and the Philippians. In Ephesians we had the emphasis on the fact that the church is the body of Christ down here in the world. The emphasis was upon the body. In Colossians the emphasis is upon the head of the body, the person of the Lord Jesus Christ. In Ephesians we read, "And hath put all things under his feet, and gave him to be the head over all things to the church" (Eph. 1:22). And finally, in Philippians we see the church with feet, walking through the world—we see the experience of the church, the experience of the believer. These are companion epistles.

"The firstborn from the dead." Did you know that there is only one Man who has been raised in a glorified body today? He is the firstfruits of them that sleep. When a loved one who is in Christ dies and you put that body into the grave, you are just putting it into a motel. It is like putting it into a hotel for a few days, because there is a bright morning coming. The body is put to sleep, but the individual has gone to be with the Lord. When Christ comes to take His church out of this world, then that body is going to be raised on the basis of His resurrection. It is sown in corruption, but it will be raised in incorruption (see 1 Cor. 15:42). We shall be just as He is. "Beloved, now are we the sons of God, and it doth not yet appear what we shall be: but we know that, when he shall appear, we shall be like him; for we shall see him as he is" (1 John 3:2).

8. "That in all things he might have the preeminence." You cannot think of anything more wonderful than this. The will of Christ must prevail throughout all of God's creation. That is God's intention. Even in spite of the rebellion of man down here on earth, God says, "Yet have I set my king upon my holy hill of Zion" (Ps. 2:6). God is moving forward today undeviatingly, unhesitatingly, uncompromisingly toward one goal. That goal is to put Jesus on the throne of this world which today is in rebellion against God. That is the objective of God.

For it pleased the Father that in him should all fulness dwell [Col. 1:19].

9. "It pleased the Father that in him should all fulness dwell." The fullness is the plērōma. That is one of the most important words in this epistle. Over in Philippians it was the kenōsis. That is, it emphasized that Christ emptied Himself and became a servant; He emptied Himself of the glory that He had with the Father. He didn't empty Himself of His deity—He was God when He came to this earth. The plērōma, the full fullness of God, dwells in Him.

When He was down here on this earth, the plērōma was at home in Jesus. He was 100 percent God—not 99.44 percent, but 100 percent. That little baby that was lying on the bosom of Mary over nineteen hundred years ago seemed so helpless, but He could have spoken this universe out of existence. He is Man of very man; He is God of very God. That is who He is.

We can outline these verses from another perspective. I would like to do this for you in order to add to our understanding of this portion of Scripture.

1. Christ's relationship to the Father—verse 15
2. Christ's relationship to creation—verses 16–17
3. Christ's relationship to the church—verses 18–19
4. Christ's relationship to the cross—verse 20

OBJECTIVE WORK OF CHRIST FOR SINNERS

We are going to see here the things Christ has done for us.

And, having made peace through the blood of his cross, by him to reconcile all things unto himself; by him, I say, whether they be things in earth, or things in heaven [Col. 1:20].

"Having made peace through the blood of his cross" means that by His paying the penalty on the cross for your sin and my sin, peace has been made between God and the sinner. God does not approach man today and say to him, "Look here, fellow, I'm against you. You have been rebelling against Me. You are a sinner, and I am forced to punish you for that." No, God is saying something entirely different to the lost sinner today. He says to you and to me, "I have already borne the punishment, I have already paid the penalty for all your sin. I want you to know that you can come to Me. Peace has already been made in Christ Jesus, if you will just turn and come to Me."

This is what Paul meant when he wrote, "Therefore being justified by faith, we have peace with God through our Lord Jesus Christ" (Rom. 5:1). Peace has been made through the *blood* of His cross. Paul puts forgiveness of sin right along with the blood of the cross. God can forgive because the penalty has already been paid. Jesus paid that penalty through the blood of His cross; therefore a righteous God can forgive you. God is not a disagreeable neighbor who is waiting around the corner to pounce on the sinner and to find fault with him. God has His arms outstretched and is saying, "Come, and I will give you redemption rest."

"By him to reconcile all things unto himself." Reconciliation is toward man; redemption is toward God. God is saying to all men today, "I am reconciled to you. Now will you be reconciled to Me?" That is the decision a man must make.

Paul explains this very clearly in his letter to the Corinthians. "And all things are of God, who hath reconciled us to himself by Jesus Christ, and hath given to us the ministry of reconciliation; To wit, that God was in Christ, reconciling the world unto himself, not imputing their trespasses unto them; and hath committed unto us the word of reconciliation. Now then we are ambassadors for Christ, as though God did beseech you by us: we pray you in Christ's stead, be ye reconciled to God" (2 Cor. 5:18–20).

A great many people have the idea that a man must do something to win God over to him. My friend, God is trying to win you over—the shoe is on the other foot. God is reconciled. He is asking man to be reconciled to Him.

"Reconcile all things"—some people take this statement and get the foolish notion that everybody is going to be saved. To understand this we need to pay a little attention to the grammar that is here. What are the "all things"? We will see that it is limited to all things that are to be reconciled, those which are appointed for reconciliation.

Maybe it would help us if we look at Philippians 3:8 where Paul says, "Yea doubtless, and I count all things but loss for the excellency of the knowledge of Christ Jesus my Lord. . . ." What are the "all things" here? Does Paul include everything in the whole world? No, it refers to all the things that Paul had to lose. In the verses just previous Paul had enumerated all the religious pluses which he had had in his life. It is all these things which Paul counted for loss. Paul couldn't lose something that he didn't have.

"Whether they be things in earth, or things in heaven." You will notice that Paul limits the "all things" that are appointed to reconciliation—he doesn't mention things under the earth. In Ephesians 1:22 it says, "And hath put all things under his feet, and gave him to be the head over all things to the church." What are the "all things" that are going to be put under His feet? Well, in Philippians Paul wrote, "That at the name of Jesus every knee should bow, of things in heaven, and things in earth, and things under the earth" (Phil. 2:10). Notice that all things are going to acknowledge the lordship of Jesus Christ—all things in heaven, in earth, and under the earth. That doesn't mean that they are all reconciled. Paul makes no mention of things under the earth being reconciled to God.

My friend, don't listen to the deception, the siren song, that all is going to work out well. Don't think you can depend on God being nice and sweet and pleasant like a little old lady. Things in heaven and in earth are reconciled to God, but not the things under the earth. The things under the earth will have to bow to Him, but they are not reconciled to Him at all. This is the place and this is the life in which we need to be reconciled to God.

"Things in heaven"—not only must we be made ready for heaven, but heaven must be made ready to receive us. The Lord Jesus said, ". . . I go to prepare a place for you" (John 14:2). By the Incarnation God came down to man; by the blood of Jesus man is brought up to God. This blood also purifies things in heaven according to Hebrews 9:23–24. Heaven must also be reconciled.

And you, that were sometimes alienated and enemies in your mind by wicked works, yet now hath he reconciled [Col. 1:21].

God did not wait until we promised to scrub our faces, put on our Sunday clothes, and go to Sunday school before He agreed to do this work of reconciliation. It was while you and I were in rebellion against Him, while we were doing wicked works, that He reconciled us to Himself. No man can say, "I'm lost because God has not made adequate provision for me." A man is lost because he wants to be lost, because he is in rebellion against God.

"That were sometime alienated and enemies in your mind." This reminds us that there is a *mental* alienation from God as well as a moral alienation. A great many people think that men are lost because they have committed some terrible sin. The reason people are lost is that their minds are alienated from God. I think this explains the fierce antagonism toward God on the part of the so-called intellectuals of our day. There is an open hatred and hostility toward God.

Some time ago I had the funeral of a certain movie star out here in California. The Hollywood crowd came to the funeral. One of the television newscasters commented on the funeral, and I appreciated what he had to say about it. He said, "Today Hollywood heard something that it had never heard before." But I also saw something there at that funeral that I had never seen before. I had never seen so much hatred in the eyes of men and women as I saw when I attempted to present Jesus Christ and to explain how wonderful He is and how He wants to save people. There is an alienation in the mind and heart of man.

In the body of his flesh through death, to present you holy and unblameable and unreproveable in his sight [Col. 1:22].

"The body of his flesh"—here is an explicit declaration that Christ suffered—not just in appearance—but He suffered in a real body. This directly countered one of the heresies of Gnosticism in Paul's day.

"To present you holy and unblameable and unreproveable in his sight." *Unblameable* means "without blemish." That was the requirement of the sacrificial animal in the Old Testament. You and I cannot present perfection to God, and God cannot accept anything short of perfection. That is the reason we cannot be saved by our works or by our character. We simply cannot meet the demands of a righteous God. But He is able to present us unblameable. Why? Because He took our place. "For he hath made him to be sin for us, who knew no sin; that we might be made the righteousness of God in him" (2 Cor. 5:21).

Unreproveable means "unaccusable or unchargeable." God is the One who justified us. If God declares us to be justified, who can bring any kind of a charge against us? He is the One who has cleared us of all guilt.

If ye continue in the faith grounded and settled, and be not moved away from the hope of the gospel, which ye have heard, and which was preached to every creature which is under heaven; whereof I Paul am made a minister [Col. 1:23].

This is not a conditional clause that is based on the future. The *if* that Paul uses here is the *if* of argument. It does not mean that something *shall be* if something else is true; rather it means that something *was* if something else is true. We would say, "*Since* ye continue in the faith grounded and settled." Paul's point is that we have been reconciled—it is an accomplished fact. So if you are a child of God today, you will continue in the faith grounded and settled. You will not be moved away from the hope of the gospel which you have heard.

"Whereof I Paul am made a minister." Paul loved to look back and rest in his glorious privilege of being a minister of Jesus Christ. I consider that the greatest honor that can come to any person. I thank God every day for the privilege that He has given me of declaring His Word—there is nothing quite like that.

SUBJECTIVE WORK OF CHRIST FOR SAINTS

Who now rejoice in my sufferings for you, and fill up that which is behind of the afflictions of Christ in my flesh for his body's sake, which is the church [Col. 1:24].

Let me give you a free translation of this verse. "Now I, Paul, rejoice in the midst of my sufferings for you, and I am filling up in my flesh that which is lacking of the afflictions of Christ for his body's sake, which is the church." Paul is saying here that it was necessary for him to fill up in suffering that which was lacking in the suffering of Christ. Isn't that a startling statement? Someone will say, "Doesn't that contradict what you have been teaching all along? You say Christ suffered for us and paid the penalty and there is nothing we can do for salvation." That is very true, and this verse does not contradict that at all.

Paul was suffering in his body for the sake of Christ's body. The implication seems to be that there was something lacking in the sufferings of Christ. A second implication could be that it was necessary for Paul, and I think in turn for all believers, to make up that which is lacking. In other words, when Paul suffers for them, it completes the suffering of Christ.

All of this is rather startling because we have just called attention to the fact that this epistle teaches the fullness of Christ. "For in him dwelleth all the fulness of the Godhead bodily" (Col. 2:9). Everything is centered in Him. He is to have the preeminence in all things. Yet here it would seem that there is still something to be done.

Paul is writing this epistle from prison, and he says he has fulfilled all his sufferings. You may remember that the Lord Jesus revealed to Ananias the reason He had saved Paul and how He was going to use him. "But the Lord said unto him [Ananias], Go thy way: for he [Paul] is a chosen vessel unto me, to bear my name before the Gentiles, and kings, and the children of Israel: For I will shew him how great things he must suffer for my name's sake" (Acts 9:15–16). Now Paul writes from prison and says that he has fulfilled that.

In our discussion of this verse I want to make one thing very, very clear. The sufferings of Paul were *not redemptive*. There was no merit in his suffering for others or even for himself as concerning redemption. Paul is very careful in his selection of words here. When Paul speaks of the redemption of Christ, he does not speak of suffering but of a cross, a death, and His blood.

There are two kinds of suffering. There is *ministerial* suffering and there is *mediatorial* suffering. Christ's suffering for us was mediatorial. Actually, we can consider the sufferings of Christ and divide them into two further classifications. There is a sharp distinction between them. We will do that to clarify this passage of Scripture.

1. There are the sufferings of Christ which He endured and in which we cannot share.

He suffered as a man. He endured *human suffering*. He bore the suffering that is common to humanity when He was born in Bethlehem at His incarnation over nineteen hundred years ago. When He was born, did He cry like other little babies that come into the world? I have wondered about that, and I rather think that He did. He was clad in the garment of that frail flesh that you and I have. He could get hungry. He could become thirsty. He experienced loneliness. He suffered anguish and pain and sorrow. He could go to sleep in the boat because He was weary and tired. Those are human sufferings. We all have those.

Paul wrote, "For every man shall bear his own burden" (Gal. 6:5). There are certain burdens we must each bear alone. We are born alone. So was our Lord. We feel pain alone. There are certain problems in life that each of us must face, and we face them alone. There is a sorrow that comes that no one can share with us. We become sick, and no one can take our place.

When my daughter was just a little girl I remember crossing the desert of Arizona coming back from the East. It was the hot summertime, and she had been sick. My wife took her temperature, and it was up to 104 degrees. We took her to the hospital in Phoenix. As she was lying there with that high temperature, I would have given anything in the world at that moment if I could have taken her place. I would gladly have taken that fever for her, but I couldn't do it. We can't share such things.

There will come a time when you and I will go down through the valley of the shadow of death. Humanly speaking, we will each die alone. That is the reason it is so wonderful to be a Christian and to know that Jesus is with us at that time when no one else can go through death with us.

Jesus Christ suffered human suffering. That is a suffering which cannot be shared.

The second suffering which He could not share was His *suffering as the Son of God*. He is God, yet He identified Himself with mankind. No mortal has ever had to endure what He went through. He was made like unto His brethren, and He suffered; but He suffered as the Son of God.

We see this suffering in Psalm 69. It tells us in verses 11 and 12 that He was the song of the drunkards in that little town of Nazareth. And He said that He made sackcloth His garment. Oh, what He suffered because He was the Son of God! He was arrested. The soldiers of the high priest mocked Him. They put a robe on Him and a crown of thorns. They played a Roman game known as "Hot Hand" in which they blindfolded Him and then all the soldiers would hit Him with their fists. One of the soldiers would not hit Him, and when they removed the blindfold He was supposed to say which one had not. Even if He named the right one, they would never have admitted that He was right. Then they would put the blindfold on and play the game again. They all pounded Him until the Lord Jesus Christ was marred more than any man. They had beaten His face to a pulp before they ever put Him on the cross. He suffered in a way that no other man has suffered, because He suffered as the Son of God.

And then He *suffered as the sacrifice for the sin of the world.* He is the Lamb of God who takes away the sin of the world, and none of us can enter into that suffering at all. We can appropriate His death for us, we can recognize the fact that He took our place, but we cannot enter into it. He alone went to the cross. He was forsaken of God and forsaken by men. His was not the blood of martyrdom; His was the blood of sacrifice.

In His first three hours on the cross, man did his worst. It was light from nine o'clock until noon; man was there at his evil worst. In the second three hours, from noon until three o'clock, it was dark; that was when God was doing His best. At that time the cross became an altar on which the Lamb of God was slain to take away the sin of the world. "For Christ also hath once suffered for sins, the just for the unjust . . ." (1 Pet. 3:18). That's a suffering that you and I cannot bear; He could not share that with anyone else.

2. On the other hand, there are the sufferings Christ endured which we can share. These are the sufferings which Paul refers to in verse 24.

There is the *suffering for righteousness' sake.* In the synagogue in Nazareth, His own hometown, Jesus said, "But now ye seek to kill me, a man that hath told you the truth . . ." (John 8:40). He suffered for righteousness' sake, and we are told very definitely that we will do the same: "But and if ye suffer for righteousness' sake, happy are ye . . ." (1 Pet. 3:14). Paul wrote to young Timothy: "Yea, and all that will live godly in Christ Jesus shall suffer persecution" (2 Tim. 3:12).

May I say to you that if you are going to live for God, if you are going to take a stand for the right, you will find that you will be passed by. God's men are passed by today in the distribution of earthly honors. The world will damn the man of God with faint praise, and they will praise him with faint damns. That is the way the world treats God's men today. Athletes are lauded, people in the entertainment world are praised, politicians are praised, and professors are honored; but the man of God is not praised. If you stand for the things that are right in this world, you will suffer for righteousness' sake. Paul understood this, and he wrote, "As it is written, For thy sake we are killed all the day long; we are accounted as sheep for the slaughter" (Rom. 8:36). That will be the lot of anyone who stands for God.

Then there is the *suffering in the measure we identify ourselves with Christ for the proclamation of the gospel.* John wrote, ". . . because as he is, so are we in this world" (1 John 4:17). The Lord Jesus made it very clear, "If the world hate you, ye know that it hated me before it hated you. If ye were of the world, the world would love his own: but because ye are not of the world, but I have chosen you out of the world, therefore the world hateth you" (John 15:18–19). If you are not of the world, the world *will* hate you.

The popularity of the Christian with the world is in inverse ratio to his popularity with Christ. If you are popular with the world as a Christian, then you are not popular with Christ. If you are going to be popular with Christ, you are not going to be popular in this world. The child of God is to take his rightful place and identify himself with Christ. When we suffer for Christ, the Lord Jesus is also suffering through us, through His church.

You remember when the Lord Jesus appeared to Saul on the road to Damascus, He said, ". . . Saul, Saul, why persecutest thou me?" (Acts 9:4). That young Pharisee was startled and puzzled. Saul of Tarsus thought that he was persecuting Christians. He was shocked to learn that he wa actually persecuting the Lord Jesus Christ.

This is what Peter wrote about our suffering: "Beloved, think it not strange concerning the fiery trial which is to try you, as though some strange thing happened unto you: But rejoice, inasmuch as ye are partakers of Christ's sufferings; that, when his glory shall be revealed, ye may be glad also with exceeding joy" (1 Pet. 4:12–13).

There is one thing for certain: If the gospel is to go forward today, someone must suffer. The late Dr. George Gill said that when a child is born into this world, some woman must travail in pain; and the reason there are not more people being born again is because there are not enough believers who are willing to travail. Suffering is not popular—but that is what Paul is talking about in this verse.

All of us would like to see revival. We talk glibly about witnessing and about living for God and all that sort of thing. My friend, may I say to you that if the gospel is going to go forward today and if people are going to be saved, someone is going to have to pay a price. How much are you paying to get out the Word of God? What is it really costing you? Are you willing to suffer for the sake of the gospel?

Whereof I am made a minister, according to the dispensation of God which is given to me for you, to fulfil the word of God [Col. 1:25].

The word *dispensation* means economy—even by transliteration; it is a stewardship. We talk of political economy, domestic economy, business economy. God deals with the world on the basis of different economies or stewardships, but they have always been based on the redemption which is in Christ Jesus. Before Jesus was born into this world, men brought a little lamb as a sacrifice, and they looked forward to the coming of Christ. They were not saved by that little lamb; but they brought the lamb in faith, and they were saved by the Christ who would some day die for them. That was the economy or the stewardship which God has set for the Jews in the Old Testament. We don't bring a little lamb for a sacrifice today because it is now an historical fact that Christ has already come. All we have to do today is trust Him.

"The dispensation of God which is given to me for you," Paul writes to the gentile people in Colosse. They are a part of this new dispensation. The Gentiles are to be included in the church.

"To fulfil the word of God." This was something that had been hidden in the Old Testament, but now God has declared that the gospel must go to the Gentiles.

Even the mystery which hath been laid from ages and from generations, but now is made manifest to his saints [Col. 1:26].

A "mystery" is something that had not been revealed in the Old Testament but is now revealed. We learn in Ephesians that the mystery was not the fact that Gentiles would be saved—that was known in the Old Testament. The mystery, the new thing, was that God would now put Israel on the same basis as the Gentiles. All men are lost; all men have sinned; all men have come short of the glory of God. Now God is taking both Jews and Gentiles, men out of all races, and He is putting them into a new body which is called the church. That was never revealed in the Old Testament, but it is now being revealed.

"Now is made manifest to his saints"—Paul wasn't the only one who understood this mystery. God was making it known to His saints in that day.

> **To whom God would make known what is the riches of the glory of this mystery among the Gentiles; which is Christ in you, the hope of glory [Col. 1:27].**

"Christ in you, the hope of glory"—we are in Christ. The moment you put your trust in Christ Jesus, the Holy Spirit baptizes you and puts you in the body of believers. You and I have been brought into something new, the church, and the church has a glorious prospect ahead of it.

> **Whom we preach, warning every man, and teaching every man in all wisdom; that we may present every man perfect in Christ Jesus [Col. 1:28].**

"Whom we preach." The gospel is not *what* we preach, but it is *whom* we preach. No man has ever preached the gospel who hasn't preached Christ. Jesus Christ is the gospel. He is eternal life. John wrote that he was going to show us eternal life, that he had seen eternal life (see 1 John 1:1–2). Whom had John seen? He'd seen Christ. And, my friend, today you either have Him or you don't have Him. The gospel is Christ—what He has done for us in His death and resurrection and what He is going to do in the future.

"Warning every man, and teaching every man in all wisdom." I believe there are two commands here for ministers today—these are two things we should be doing. We are to preach the gospel in order to win sinners to Christ and to save them from the wrath that is to come, and we are to teach every man in all wisdom. In other words, we are to seek to build up men and women so that they may grow in grace and be faithful members of the body of Christ; they are to be encouraged to serve Christ in the local assembly.

I am told that my teaching of the Bible helps the local churches, and that is the reason I have the support of so many pastors across this country. If I am not doing that, then I would have to say I am not ful- filling my ministry.

"That we may present every man perfect in Christ Jesus." *Perfect* actually means "complete or mature." This is the goal of the teaching of the Word of God.

> **Whereunto I also labour, striving according to his work- ing, which worketh in me mightily [Col. 1:29].**

Striving means "to agonize." Paul is giving us his very personal testi- mony: "This is what I'm laboring, striving to do."

"According to his working, which worketh in me mightily." Oh, this should be the desire of everyone today who is working for Christ—that He would work in us mightily to do two things: to get out the gospel that men might be saved and then to build them up in the faith. These are the two things the church should be doing today.

CHAPTER 2

THEME: Christ, the answer to philosophy; Christ, the answer to ritual

In the first fifteen verses of this chapter we will see that Christ is the answer to philosophy. The remainder of the chapter will show that He is the answer to ritual. The answer to philosophy is for the head; the answer to ritual is for the heart.

Christianity has always been in the danger of sailing between Scylla and Charybdis. On one extreme Christianity is in danger of evaporating into a philosophy—then it becomes nothing but steam. The opposite danger is that it will freeze into a form and become nothing more than a ritual. There is a real peril on either side. But the Lord Jesus called Himself the *Water* of Life. He is neither steam nor ice—neither can sustain life. That is why we need to guard against following the line of philosophy or following the line of ritual. Christianity is Christ!

There were five errors that endangered the Colossian church which Paul will deal with in this chapter. They were:

1. Enticing words—verses 4–7
2. Philosophy—verses 8–13
3. Legality—verses 14–17
4. Mysticism—verses 18–19
5. Asceticism—verses 20–23

These are still dangers today. I think that most of us could sit down with this chapter and go through it to make an inventory of our spiritual lives. It would show us the direction in which we are going. A great many even so-called Bible believers have slipped into one or more of these errors.

CHRIST, THE ANSWER TO PHILOSOPHY
(For the Head)

For I would that ye knew what great conflict I have for you, and for them at Laodicea, and for as many as have not seen my face in the flesh [Col. 2:1].

Laodicea was near to Colosse. I have been to Laodicea but not to Colosse. Yet I stood on the high point of Laodicea and looked across the Lycos valley. There alongside the mountains at the gates of Phrygia, which lead into the Orient, were the ruins of Colosse. It was a great city, but it was not nearly as great as Laodicea. In Laodicea was one of the seven churches of the Book of Revelation; it was the church that is described as being lukewarm.

"Conflict" is our word *agony*. MacPhail calls this a prayer of agony. Paul saw that there was a grave danger in Colosse and in Laodicea, and it caused great conflict in the heart of the apostle. They were in danger of going off in one of two directions. There is still such danger, and we need a lot of agonizing prayer for the church today. This explains why we find the Laodiceans' lukewarm condition in the Book of Revelation: they had lost sight of the person of Christ. Christ is the answer to man's head; He is also the answer to man's heart.

"For as many as have not seen my face in the flesh." Colosse is located about 100 miles inland from ancient Ephesus. When Paul came through that area (which he did twice), he did not come down to Colosse and Laodicea. Even when he attempted to go down into Asia on his second missionary journey, the Spirit of God forbade him; so he turned and took the northern route. Then when he came on his third missioanry journey, walking over the land, he again took the northern route, perhaps because he was already familiar with it. It is clear that he had not been to these cities because he writes, "and for as many as have not seen my face in the flesh." This might be interpreted to mean that many new believers had come into the church since he had been there and that they had not seen his face. That meaning is highly unlikely; I think it means that Paul had never been there.

That their hearts might be comforted, being knit together in love, and unto all riches of the full assurance of understanding, to the acknowledgement of the mystery of God, and of the Father, and of Christ [Col. 2:2].

"That their hearts might be comforted." *Heart* indicates the entire inner man. That means the whole propulsive nature of man. He is praying that their hearts, their humanity, their whole persons might be comforted.

"Being knit together in love" means compacted in love. Love will draw them together. After all, a church is not united by gifts or even by what we term today as spirituality. The bond that unites believers is love. It is the cement that holds us together—it is the Elmer's glue of the church.

"Unto all riches of the full assurance of understanding." *Full assurance* is an interesting expression; it literally means "to be under full sail." It means that believers should be moving along spiritually—they should be moving along for God.

"To the acknowledgement of the mystery of God, and of the Father, and of Christ." I grant that is a rather awkward expression, and a better translation would be: "the mystery of God, even of the Father, and of Christ." Better and easier yet might be, "the mystery of God, even Christ." I think that is the correct meaning of it.

What is "the mystery of God, even Christ"? The church is the mystery, for it had not been revealed in the Old Testament. God was going to save Gentiles—that had been made clear in the Old Testament, and He did save them. But on the Day of Pentecost God started a *new* thing. He began to call out a group of people into the body of believers, baptized by the Spirit of God into this body. This is what Paul is explaining in 1 Corinthians 12:12: "For as the body is one, and hath many members, and all the members of that one body, being many, are one body: so also is Christ." You see, Christ had a physical body while He was here on this earth, and He has a spiritual body down here today. That body is the body of believers that have trusted Him, and the body is called Christ." That is why the Lord said to Saul of Tarsus. "Why are you persecuting me?" (see Acts 9:4). Saul was persecuting Him per-

sonally. The church is Christ—it belongs to Him. "The mystery of God, even Christ."

In 1 Corinthians 12:13, Paul goes on to say of the church: "For by one Spirit are we all baptized into one body, whether we be Jews or Gentiles, whether we be bond or free; and have been all made to drink into one Spirit." We have all been baptized into Christ. We have all been made to drink into one Spirit. That is what brings the unity into the church. We are never commanded to make a unity of the church. It is impossible to join some organization and to expect that organization to bring about church unity. The Holy Spirit has already made that unity. He puts all believers into one body, and we are told to keep the unity of the Spirit. Our problem today is that we are not keeping the unity of the Spirit.

In whom are hid all the treasures of wisdom and knowledge [Col. 2:3].

All that we need is in Christ. If only we could learn that! He is the reservoir of all knowledge.

In the science building where I went to college there was a motto on the bulletin board. It hung there the whole time that I was in college, and it made a great impression on me. I'm afraid I remember it better than I do the sciences that I studied there. It said, "Next to knowing is knowing where to find out." I love that. I willingly admit that I don't know everything—I'm sure you have found that out by now. But I know where to find out, because I know Somebody who does know. Christ has been made unto us wisdom. We need to rest in that. All the treasures of wisdom and knowledge are in Him—how wonderful this is!

1. Now Paul will discuss the error of *enticing words.*

And this I say, lest any man should beguile you with enticing words [Col. 2:4].

He is going to deal with the matter of philosophy and enticing words. Philosophy and psychology have been substituted for the Bible, and this is the thing that is enticing to so many young preachers in our seminaries today. I am amazed to find that some of these men with a Ph.D. degree from a seminary know so little about the Bible! They know all about Bultmann and Kant and Plato, but they don't seem to know very much about the Word of God. That is the great problem of our day.

There was that same danger in Colosse and also in Laodicea. I think that is what actually killed the church in Colosse, and it made the church in Laocidea the weakest of the seven churches in Asia Minor. It was in the worst spiritual condition, and yet the people thought that they were well off. These cities were wealthy. They boasted of their wealth and affluence and also of their knowledge, but they were blind to their true spiritual condition.

Paul says, "Don't let any man beguile you with enticing words." *Beguile* means "to victimize." *Enticing words* are a lot of oratory or sweet-talk.

I heard of a theologian who uses big words and tries to be very deep in his thinking. He was talking to a group of men for about half an hour. Another man walked up to the group and asked one of the men on the outside of the circle, "What's he talking about?" The fellow answered, "He hasn't said yet." That is the problem—he never would say. All he did was talk with enticing words.

I know a dear lady who attends a certain church because, as she says, "I just love to go there because the preacher uses such flowery language and he makes me feel so good all over." That is the danger today. A great many people love this pretense toward intellectuality among preachers rather than the simple Word of God.

I started preaching before I went to college, and then in college I was exposed to liberalism because I went to a liberal college. That was all I knew at that time; I was not grounded in the Word of God at all, even though I had had a wonderful pastor. I thought I wanted to be an intellectual preacher—I thought that would be great. I thank God that that was knocked out of me in my second year of college. I became concerned with teaching the Word of God.

Paul warns us to beware that they will beguile us with enticing words and will victimize us. Their words cause many people to follow a certain individual instead of the Word of God. Like the Pied Piper of Hamlin, he starts playing, and the unwary start following.

For though I be absent in the flesh, yet am I with you in the spirit, joying and beholding your order, and the stedfastness of your faith in Christ [Col. 2:5].

At this time the word that was coming back to Paul was that this church *was* standing.

"Beholding your order." *Order* is a military term, and it means "to stand shoulder to shoulder." That is what believers ought to be doing—standing shoulder to shoulder. Instead, many today are trying to undermine or take advantage of another believer. Oh that we could stand shoulder to shoulder with one another!

Stedfastness means "to have a solid front, to be immovable." The literal translation would be "stereotype," or the opposite of movable type. Paul writes this same thought to the Corinthians: "Therefore, my beloved brethren, be ye stedfast, unmoveable, always abounding in the work of the Lord, forasmuch as ye know that your labour is not in vain in the Lord" (1 Cor. 15:58). The Colossian church had a reputation for steadfastness, and Paul wanted them to continue like that and not be led away by the oratory of some.

As ye have therefore received Christ Jesus the Lord, so walk ye in him [Col. 2:6].

What does it mean to be saved, to be a Christian? Well, I have a letter from a man who tells me that I am not saved because I have frankly admitted that I am not perfect, that I do not keep all the Ten Commandments. He says that I am not saved until I do. My friend, salvation is to receive a person, and that person is Jesus Christ—"As ye have therefore received Christ Jesus the Lord."

"So walk ye in him." Now that you have received Him, *walk* in Him, walk in the Spirit. Walking is not a balloon ascension. A great many people think the Christian life is some great, overwhelming experience and you take off like a rocket going out into space. That's not where you live the Christian life. Rather, it is in your home, in your office, in the schoolroom, on the street. The way you get around in this life is to *walk*. You are to walk in Christ. God grant that you and I might be joined to Him in our daily walk.

> **Rooted and built up in him, and stablished in the faith, as ye have been taught, abounding therein with thanksgiving [Col. 2:7].**

"Rooted" means rooted like a tree, and a tree is a living thing. And we are to be "built up" as a house. A house is not a living thing, but it requires a tremendous foundation. Paul tells us in Ephesians that the foundation is Jesus Christ. Having received Christ, we are to walk in Him. Doing what? Being rooted, drawing our life from Him as a tree, and built up in Him, your faith resting upon Him.

That is why he adds, "and stablished in the faith." A better translation would be "by your faith." Faith is the means by which you and I lay hold of Christ.

2. Now Paul moves on to discuss the danger of *philosophy*.

> **Beware lest any man spoil you through philosophy and vain deceit, after the tradition of men, after the rudiments of the world, and not after Christ [Col. 2:8].**

"Beware"—Look out! Stop, look, and listen!

"Lest any man spoil you through philosophy and vain deceit." If you were to follow the history of philosophy beginning with Plato, including many of the church fathers, and coming down to more recent times (including Kant, Locke, and Bultmann, who seems to be the craze with some theologians right now), you would find that none of them have a high view of the inspiration of the Word of God. They are looking for answers to the problems of life, but they will not be found in philosophy.

A true philosopher is a seeker after truth, but truth is not found in human wisdom. Christ is the answer, the answer to philosophy. Paul wrote, "But of him are ye in Christ Jesus, *who of God is made unto us wisdom . . ."* (1 Cor. 1:30, italics mine). But false philosophy is like a blind man looking in a dark room for a black cat that isn't there—there is no hope for its search for truth. Paul warns the Colossians to beware of this.

"After the tradition of men." You may remember that the Lord Jesus condemned the religious rulers in His day because they taught the tradition of men rather than the Word of God. Very frankly, this is one of the reasons I have turned to the teaching of the total Word of God. It is so easy to lift out some peculiar interpretation of some particular passage and then ride that like a hobby horse. I believe in prophecy, but there is more in the Word of God than just prophecy. Some preachers dwell on the Christian life. That certainly is in the Bible, but there is more than just that. This is why I think it is so important for us to study the *total* Word of God.

"After the rudiments of the world, and not after Christ." The Greek word for "rudiments" is *stoicheion*, which means "that which is basic," the ABC's. Some people try to build their Christian living on some worldly system that seems so simple. Our base is not philosophy or a worldly system; our base is Christ.

Now Paul will speak of Christ:

> **For in him dwelleth all the fulness of the Godhead bodily [Col. 2:9].**

In Him dwelleth all the *plerōma*—this is a clear-cut statement of the deity of Christ. It could not be stated any stronger than it is here. In Him dwells *all* the fullness of the Godhead—not just 99.44 percent but 100 percent.

> **And ye are complete in him, which is the head of all principality and power [Col. 2:10].**

You "are complete in him." "Complete" is a nautical term, and it could be translated in this very vivid way: You are ready for the voyage of life in Him. Isn't that a wonderful way of saying it? You are ready for the voyage of life in Christ, and whatever you need for the voyage of life you will find in Him. This is where we say that Christ is the answer. What is your question? What is it you need today? Are you carried away by human philosophy? Then turn to Christ. Are you carried away by enticing words? Are you carried away by the systems and traditions of men? Turn to Christ.

> **In whom also ye are circumcised with the circumcision made without hands, in putting off the body of the sins of the flesh by the circumcision of Christ [Col. 2:11].**

Paul is telling them to get rid of that which is outward. The real circumcision is the New Birth. He explained this to the Galatians: "For in Christ Jesus neither circumcision availeth any thing, nor uncircumcision, but a new creature" (Gal. 6:15). You and I become new creatures when we come to Christ and trust Him as our Savior. We rest in Him; we are identified with Him.

> **Buried with him in baptism, wherein also ye are risen with him through the faith of the operation of God, who hath raised him from the dead [Col. 2:12].**

Lord Lyndhurst was the Lord Chancellor of Great Britain and possessed a sharp legal mind. He made this statement: "I know pretty well what evidence is; and I tell you, such evidence as that for the Resurrection has never broken down yet." The death and resurrection of Christ is an historical fact. When Christ died you and I died with Him; He took our place. And when He was raised, we were raised in Him, and we are now joined to a living Christ. It is so important for us to see that we are joined to a living Savior.

It is so important to keep in mind that no outward ceremony brings us to Christ. The issue is whether or not we are born again, whether we really know Christ as Savior. If we do know Him, we are identified with Him. Identification with Christ is "putting off the body of the sins of the flesh by the circumcision of Christ," which is a spiritual circumcision.

When you put your trust in the Lord Jesus Christ, the Holy Spirit baptizes you into the body of Christ. It is by this baptism that we are identified with Christ, and we are also "risen with him"—joined to the living Christ.

"Through the faith of the operation of God who hath raised him from the dead"—salvation is accomplished by the resurrection power of God. It's not some philosophy; it's not some gimmick; it's not some little system; it's not the taking of some course that will enable you to live for God.

And you, being dead in your sins and the uncircumcision of your flesh, hath he quickened together with him, having forgiven you all trespasses [Col. 2:13].

Salvation is not the improvement of the old nature; it is the impartation of a new nature.

Remember that Paul had to deal with two systems of Greek philosophy which were very popular in his day. They were diametrically opposed to each other, but they both came out at the same end of the horn. One philosophy was Stoicism, and the other was Epicureanism.

The Stoic taught that man was to live nobly and that death could not matter. The idea was to hold the appetites in check and to become indifferent to changing conditions. In effect they said, "Be not uplifted by good fortune nor cast down by adversity." They believed that man is more than circumstances and that the soul is greater than the universe. It was a brave philosophy, you see. But the problem was how to live it. It was like the people who say that they are living by the Sermon on the Mount when actually they are many miles from it.

The Epicurean taught that all is uncertain. "We know not whence we came; we know not whither we go. We only know that after a brief life we disappear from this scene, and it is vain to deny ourselves any present joy in view of the possible future ill. Let us eat and drink, for tomorrow we die."

The interesting thing to observe is that both these systems attempted to deal with the flesh—that is, the old nature that you and I have—not the meat on our bones. The old nature works through our old habits, old desires, old testings and temptations. How are we going to bring that under control?

There are all kinds of gimmicks and systems that are set before us today to enable us to live the Christian life. I know people who have been to Bible conferences where the Christian life is taught, and at home they have a drawer filled with notebooks. But they are not doing so well in living the Christian life. Why not? Because we need to recognize this one important thing that Paul is saying here: we are joined to the living Christ. Now, if you are joined to Him, my friend, you are going to live as if you are. How close are you to Him? Do you walk with Him? Do you turn to Him in all the emergencies of this life? Is He the One who is the very center of your life?

3. As Paul turns now to the error of *legality*, we will again find that the answer is to come to the Word of God and through it to come into a personal relationship with Jesus Christ.

> A glory gilds the sacred page,
> Majestic like the sun.
> It sheds a light on every age;
> It gives but borrows none.

Blotting out the handwriting of ordinances that was against us, which was contrary to us, and took it out of the way, nailing it to his cross [Col. 2:14].

"Blotting out the handwriting of ordinances that was against us." This old flesh of ours has been condemned. When Christ died, He died for you and me; He paid the penalty for our sin.

When the Lord Jesus died, Pilate wrote a title and put it on the cross: "This is Jesus of Nazareth the King of the Jews" (see John 19:19). He was being publicly executed on the grounds that He had led in a rebellion. This was, of course, not true, but that was the charge against Him. When the people standing there read that sign they understood that He had been disloyal to Caesar in that He had made Himself to be a king. To them that was the reason He was dying on a cross.

But when God looked upon that cross, He saw an altar on which the Lamb of God who takes away the sin of the world was offered. God saw another inscription there high above the inscription that man had written. "Blotting out the handwriting of ordinances that was against us, which was contrary to us, and took it out of the way, *nailing it to his cross.*" What did God write on that cross? He wrote the ordinances—He wrote the Ten Commandments. He wrote a law which I cannot keep, ordinances which I am guilty of breaking. When Christ died there, He did not die because He broke them; He was sinless. But it was because I broke them, because I am a sinner, and because you are. "For all have sinned, and come short of the glory of God" (Rom. 3:23).

Therefore, my friend, if God has saved you and raised you from the dead and joined you to a living Christ, why should you go back to a law that you couldn't keep in the first place? You can't even keep the law today in your own power and in your own strength. You see, the law was given to discipline the old nature. But now the believer is given a new nature, and the law has been removed as a way of life.

Let me give you an illustration. A man once came to me and said, "I'll give you $100 if you will show me where the Sabbath day has been changed." I answered, "I don't think it has been changed. Saturday is Saturday, it is the seventh day of the week, and it is the Sabbath day. I realize our calendar has been adjusted and can be off a few days, but we won't even consider that point. The seventh day is still Saturday and is still the Sabbath day." He got a gleam in his eye and said, "Then why don't you keep the Sababth day if it hasn't been changed?" I answered, "The *day* hasn't changed, but *I* have been changed. I've been given a new creation. We celebrate the first day because that is the day He rose from the grave." That is what it means when he says that the ordinances which were against us have been nailed to His cross.

> **And having spoiled principalities and powers, he made a shew of them openly, triumphing over them in it [Col. 2:15].**

The spiritual victory that Christ won for the believer is of inestimable value.

CHRIST, THE ANSWER TO RITUAL (For the Heart)

Let no man therefore judge you in meat, or in drink, or in respect of an holyday, or of the new moon, or of the sabbath days:

Which are a shadow of things to come; but the body is of Christ [Col. 2:16–17].

A believer is not to observe ordinances that are only ritual and liturgical; they have no present value. God did give certain rituals for the people in the Old Testament. So what has changed? Paul explains that they were merely "a shadow of things to come." We get our word *photograph* from the Greek word used here for "shadow." All the rituals of the Law in the Old Testament were like a negative or a picture—they were just pictures of Christ. Now that Christ has come, we have the reality. Why should we go back and look at a picture?

I remember that during the days of World War II, I performed the wedding ceremony of two wonderful young people here in Pasadena. (We knew a number of young men who went to war, and some of them gave their lives.) This young fellow was sent overseas, and while he was gone, his young bride carried the biggest purse I have ever seen (and I have seen some big ones). In that purse she carried a huge photograph of him. Most people carry a little bitty picture with them, but not this girl; she carried a photograph that you could have hung on the wall. She was everlastingly drawing it out and showing it to people. She'd say, "Isn't he handsome?" (Between you and me, he wasn't what I would call a handsome boy. He was a wonderful boy, but he was not handsome.) Then the day came when the war was over, and he was coming home. She went all the way to Seattle, Washington, to meet him. Now what do you think she did when she saw him coming down the gangplank? She hadn't seen him in a couple of years. Do you think she took out that picture and looked at it? Do you think she looked at the picture and said, "Isn't he wonderful?" I don't think she even had that picture with her! She saw *him* and when she saw him, she didn't need a picture—she threw her arms around *him*.

Many of us need to get off the merry-go-round of attending seminars, adapting gimmicks, jumping through everybody's little hoop, and taking a shortcut to the abundant life. Have we really arrived? Some think they have. Let's stop carrying around a faded photograph when we have the reality—"Christ in you, the hope of glory."

4. We come now to the warning against mysticism.

Let no man beguile you of your reward in a voluntary humility and worshipping of angels, intruding into those things which he hath not seen, vainly puffed up by his fleshly mind,

And not holding the Head, from which all the body by joints and bands having nourishment ministered, and knit together, increaseth with the increase of God [Col. 2:18–19].

This is another point at which people get off the track. Paul is here condemning the Gnostics who made a pretense of wisdom. And we have today in our church circles a great many folk who assume a pious superiority—they are what I call "spiritual snobs." It has been my experience that these people generally are very ignorant of the Bible. "Intruding into those things which he hath not seen"—that's a pretense, putting on, acting like you have something that you don't really have.

"And not holding the Head" means that such people have a loose relationship with Christ. In other words, their head is not screwed on as it should be, by the way.

5. The final warning is against the error of asceticism.

Wherefore if ye be dead with Christ from the rudiments of the world, why, as though living in the world, are ye subject to ordinances,

(Touch not; taste not; handle not;

Which all are to perish with the using;) after the commandments and doctrines of men?

> **Which things have indeed a shew of wisdom in will-worship, and humility, and neglecting of the body; not in any honour to the satisfying of the flesh [Col. 2:20–23].**

Here again, when Paul says "if ye be dead with Christ," the translation would be better as, "since ye be dead with Christ." In other words, since you have died when Christ died, do not return to pre-cross living.

I think, very candidly, that this is a terrible problem. There are people who follow some passing fad in the church. A few years ago the fad was that women couldn't use lipstick (and some of them sure looked pale). I remember when I was teaching in a school that wouldn't permit the girls to wear lipstick, a girl came to me and asked, "Do you think it is all right to use lipstick?" I answered her, "There are a lot of these folk around here who would look better if they used a little lipstick. God wants us to look the best that we can. Even when we have little to work with, we ought to do the best we can with it."

What we are dealing with here is "the pride that apes humility" that Juvenal speaks of. It is the pride that says, "I deny myself, and I don't do these things. Just look at me. I'm really sprouting wings, and I shine my halo every morning."

"Not in any honour" means it is not of any value. My friend, that is asceticism that is no good. God wants you to rejoice in Him; Christ wants you to be close to Him. And if you're going to walk with Him, my friend, you are going to have a good time!

CHAPTER 3

THEME: Christ, the fullness of God, poured out in life through believers; thoughts and affections of believers are heavenly; living of believers is holy

We come now to the line of division in this little epistle, which conforms to Paul's regular way of dividing his epistles. He always gives the doctrinal section and then the practical section. Chapters 3 and 4 comprise the practical section of Colossians.

We have seen the preeminence of Christ in chapters 1—2. We have seen Him as He is, a member of the Trinity. He is very man of very man, but He is very God of very God. He is preeminent in creation because He is the Creator. He is preeminent in redemption for He is the Redeemer. He is preeminent in the church because He is the One who gave Himself for the church.

Now we have come to the place where Paul will insist that He must be made preeminent in our lives. Today we hear a great deal of talk about dedication. Well, what is dedication? A very brief definition is: Dedication is Christ preeminent in our lives.

You cannot just say, "I am a dedicated Christian," and then live your life as you please, as a great many people are trying to do today. No, if Christ is preeminent in your life, then you are going to live out His life down here on earth. Paul has already made this clear in the doctrinal section: "For in him [in Christ] dwelleth all the fulness [plerōma] of the Godhead bodily. And ye are complete in him . . ." (Col. 2:9–10). You are made full in Him. You are ready for the voyage of life in Him. In other words, Christ is really the solution to all the problems of life.

Paul has discussed the different things that lead people away from the person of Christ. He has warned against enticing words which carry people away by great oratory. He has warned against philosophy, legality, mysticism, and asceticism. All these lead people away from the person of Christ.

The Christian life is to live out the life of Christ. You and I will find in Christ Jesus all that we need. In this practical section of the epistle, Paul will show us Christ, the fullness of God, poured out in life *through believers*—that is the only way He can be poured out.

THOUGHTS AND AFFECTIONS OF
BELIEVERS ARE HEAVENLY

If ye then be risen with Christ, seek those things which are above, where Christ sitteth on the right hand of God [Col. 3:1].

Again, this is not the *if* of condition; it is really the *if* of argument. We saw this same thing back in Colossians 1:23 where we read: "*If* ye continue in the faith grounded and settled. . . ." There was no question about their continuing in the faith grounded and settled. The lives of these Colossian Christians evidenced their salvation. What was the evidence? It was faith, hope, and love—the fruit of the Spirit was in their lives. "Since we heard of your faith in Christ Jesus"—the word had gotten around that they had a living faith in Christ Jesus; "and of the love which ye have to all the saints"—they loved the believers (Col. 1:4). Love among the believers is so important, and I do not mean this sentimental stuff that you hear so much about today. For instance, if you are a minister, you evidence your love for your congregation if you give them the Word of God, and you show your love for your pastor as a member of the church if you support his Bible-teaching ministry. My friend, love is very practical—it gets right down where the rubber meets the road. If it doesn't, it's no good at all. Love is that which manifests itself in reality. The Colossians had faith, and they had love. They also had hope: "For the hope which is laid up for you in heaven . . ." (Col. 1:5). That hope is the coming of the Lord Jesus Christ for His church. These three—faith, hope, and love—were the manifestation of the Holy Spirit in the lives of the believers in Colosse. Therefore, when Paul says, "if," it is the *if* of argument. Verse 1 here in chapter 3 would be better translated, "*Since* you are risen with Christ."

"Seek those things which are above, where Christ sitteth on the right hand of God." Where is Christ today? He's sitting at the right hand of God.

What are we to do today? We are to "seek those things which are above." Seek is an interesting word. It actually means "having an urgency and a desire and an ambition." There should be an excitement that goes with seeking spiritual things.

When we watch the Olympic games, we see folk who are running or performing some athletic feat to win a gold medal. Believe me, those folk are seeking. I don't see many saints looking for gold medals today, but we are to be seeking Christ with that kind of urgency.

"Those things which are above"—these are the things of Christ. I want you to note that Paul is not saying that we should seek such courses as are offered today that are a mixture of pseudopsychology with a smattering of Bible. This kind of teaching is handed out in a few night classes, and then some poor crippled Christians think they have the answers to the problems of life—all the way from a neurotic mother-in-law to a boss who is a dirty old man. They think some little course will teach them how to treat everybody and every problem. They consider it a do-it-yourself kit, a kind of an open sesame to a new life. Now I say to you, and I say it very carefully, you will only experience the new life as you "seek those things which are above, where Christ sitteth on the right hand of God."

I will get even more personal in my illustration. You cannot find the answers in anything I have produced—either a book or a tape-recorded message. Now I am stepping on some toes, including my own toes. A couple came to me this past summer at a conference and said, "Dr. McGee, we have a certain tape of yours, and we play it at least once a week and listen to it." My reaction was that they had better burn that tape. I had the feeling they were beginning to worship that tape and that tape wasn't getting them through to Christ.

And now I'm really going to step on toes: Paul doesn't say here to seek out and listen to any preacher or teacher! May I say this to you very kindly and very frankly: Don't make Dr. McGee or any man your idol. If you do, you have an idol who has feet of clay. You would be looking to a man who is just like you are. I make a lot of mistakes. I'm not near the man I'd like to be, nor the husband I'd like to be, nor the father or grandfather I'd like to be. Don't make anything man produces a god for yourself.

The purpose of this poor preacher is to get out the Word of God to you so that you can see the living Christ and get through to Him. If the Holy Spirit doesn't use my ministry to get you through to the living Christ, then I have failed—then I have fallen flat on my face, and I am willing to quit. I believe with all my heart that the Bible is the one Book which reveals the living Christ, and that is my purpose in teaching it.

I would like to give you an illustration of this. I went to school with a fellow who was a Canadian, and he told me about his first trip to Niagara Falls. (By the way, Mrs. McGee and I saw it for the first time this past summer. When we were looking over the falls, I said to her, "Honey, I promised you we would go to Niagara Falls on our honeymoon. I think we are still on our honeymoon, and here we are.") Well, my classmate told me that as a boy he got on a train on the Canadian side of the falls, which is the prettier side. He said, "When I got off the train, I could hear the roar of the falls, but I couldn't see them. I began to move toward the sound, and I came to a big building. I went into that building, which was like a Union Station in the United States: there was the popcorn vendor, the soda pop machine, the gift shop, and candy papers, chewing gum wrappers and even chewing gum on the floor. People were sitting all around. I was really disappointed, but I could still hear the roar of the falls. Then I looked down to the end of the building, and there I saw the biggest picture I had ever seen in my life. The frame of the picture took in most of the end of that building. It was a picture of Niagara Falls. I couldn't believe that right there at the falls they would have a picture of them. I began to walk down toward that picture, and as I drew closer to it, I began to realize that through a frame I was looking at the real, living, running Niagara Falls!"

My friend, when you read the Bible, you are not looking at a dead person. You are looking at the real, living Christ. He is the One at God's right hand. We are to seek those things which are above—we are to seek *Him*. That is why I have a ministry of teaching through the

Bible. There is no shortcut. Some have suggested that I cut it down to a one-year program, but that certainly is not adequate. And, really, five years is not adequate. Some have suggested that I lengthen it to ten years, but that is not feasible for me. Even if we took ten, or even twenty years, we would not know it all. At the end of his life Paul could still say: "That I may know him, and the power of his resurrection, and the fellowship of his sufferings, being made conformable unto his death" (Phil. 3:10).

Real study of the Word of God will get you through to the living Christ. Let me illustrate this with a letter from a listener to our radio program:

> When we were studying Romans and Corinthians, I began to realize just how much of a carnal Christian I really was. I began to desire much more than that. So I began to pray that I might truly know Christ as God would want me to. Nothing happened for a while, but I kept praying. And then God did answer my prayer. One day you said that God sees us *in Christ*, and it was as though some dark, hidden thing had been brought out into the light. I had read Ephesians many times before, but that day your message really struck home. It is a wonderful thing to know that Paul's prayer is still being answered today. I realized that day that God no longer looked down upon me as a poor sinner struggling upon this earth, but *in Christ* and that I belong to Him as a child. . . .

May I say to you from my heart, *get through to Christ.* "Seek those things which are above, where Christ sitteth at the right hand of God."

Set your affection on things above, not on things on the earth [Col. 3:2].

Actually the word for "affection" is *mind.* Think about the things that are above. In Philippians Paul said that whatever things are true and honest and just and lovely, think on these things—the things of Christ. Life is full of its smaller problems (like whether or not you can get along with your mother-in-law), and they are very real to us, but by far the greatest need is for us to get through to Christ. That should come before everything else. "Set your affection on things above."

For ye are dead, and your life is hid with Christ in God [Col. 3:3].

"For ye are dead" might better be translated "for ye have died." If you have died, *when* did you die? Paul wrote to the Galatians, "I am crucified with Christ . . ." (Gal. 2:20). You died more than nineteen hundred years ago when Christ died. He took my place; He took your place. We died in Him.

"Your life is hid with Christ in God." I have been taken out of the old Adam by baptism; that is, by the baptism of the Holy Spirit. I have been taken out of Adam and placed in Christ. I am now *in* Christ. Now that I am in Christ, I should live out His life and let His fullness be lived out through me.

When Christ, who is our life, shall appear, then shall ye also appear with him in glory [Col. 3:4].

If you have any life, it is Christ's life. John wrote in his first epistle that it was his intent to "shew unto you that eternal life." How could he show eternal life? He was going to show us Christ; Christ is eternal life. And one of these days those who belong to Him are going to "appear with him in glory."

LIVING OF BELIEVERS IS HOLY

If we are truly risen with Christ this will be evident in two areas of our lives: (1) our personal holiness, and (2) our fellowship with others who are about us.

It seems that Christians are frightened of this matter of holiness. When I was a young preacher, I heard the late Bishop Moore of the old Southern Methodist church make this statement: "If Methodists were as afraid of sin as they are of holiness, it would be a wonderful thing."

This isn't true of Methodists alone; it is true of most Christians. Somehow we don't like this term *holiness*. It is a very good word, and that is Paul's subject here—*personal holiness*.

Christ was born as a little Babe in Bethlehem, but He is no longer in that inn. He is up yonder at God's right hand at this very moment. He's on a throne—not in a cradle and not in an inn but in heaven itself. And He's there for you and me today. Now, if you are in Christ, if you have accepted Him as your Savior, then that is going to show in your life down here. Friend, if it doesn't tell in your life down here, then maybe you are not in Him up yonder!

Mortify therefore your members which are upon the earth; fornication, uncleanness, inordinate affection, evil concupiscence, and covetousness, which is idolatry [Col. 3:5].

Mortify means "to put to death, or put in the place of death."

Fornication means "sexual immorality." Is that your sin today? Let's not kid ourselves—there are a great many folk who are covering up this sin, and yet they still talk about being dedicated Christians! Paul brings this right out into the open and tells us that we are to put our physical members in the place of death. Do your eyes cause you trouble? Do you look with the eye of covetousness, or the eye of lust? Put those eyes in the place of death, and now use them as the eyes of Christ to look upon Him. My friend, that will change things, will it not?

Uncleanness includes thoughts, words, looks, gestures, and the jokes we tell.

Inordinate affection means "uncontrolled passion or lust." Every now and then someone will confess to me a sin in his life, and he will say, "Well, I couldn't help myself." My friend, you ought not to get in that spot in the first place. It's like the little boy whose mama called to him one night when she heard him in the kitchen, "Where are you?" He said, "I'm in the pantry." He had the cookie jar open. She called, "What are you doing?" He answered, "I'm fighting temptation!" My friend, that is the wrong place to fight temptation. Don't fight it there at the cookie jar, if you're not to have the cookies. The same thing applies to inordinant affection.

Evil concupiscence—that means "evil desires." Put them to death, my friend.

"Covetousness, which is idolatry" means when we always must have more. Is the almighty dollar your god today? Are you more interested in the dollar than you are in the living Christ? These questions can begin to hurt! Our bodies are the tabernacle of the Holy Spirit, and they are to be used for God.

When I drove to my office this morning there were a great many people on their way to work. Many of them were professional men and business executives. One man went by me in a Cadillac. He didn't see me or anyone else because he was in such a hurry. I don't know why he was hurrying, but I can guess. We see pictures of people in other lands going to heathen temples and worshiping there, and we feel sorry for them in the darkness of their idolatry. But I suspect that the fellow in the Cadillac was also in darkness, that he was on his way to worship his idol and to bow before it. His idol was the almighty dollar, and he was rushing to work to see how many he could make. A great many folk are overcome by this matter of covetousness. They covet the material things of this world—they want more money.

I would venture to say that covetousness is the root of most of the problems in our country today. ". . . the love of money is the root of all evil . . ." (1 Tim. 6:10). Money is not the problem—it can even be used for the glory of God. But there are many men, even Christians, who are working on that second million, and they don't need it. It is because they worship an idol. If you are in Christ, He will come first and you will seek those things which are above.

For which things' sake the wrath of God cometh on the children of disobedience [Col. 3:6].

"For which things' sake"— Paul means the things he has just been speaking of, the things which the world does.

"The wrath of God cometh on the children of disobedience." Men are not lost simply because they do these things, neither are they lost because they haven't heard of Christ. Men are lost because they are sinners, sinners in their hearts. And, because they are sinners, they do these things.

In the which ye also walked some time, when ye lived in them [Col. 3:7].

Those of us who now know the Lord practiced these sins in our lives at one time. I hope that we are not still doing them.

I met a young millionaire in Florida quite a few years ago. He very frankly admitted that before he was saved he worshiped the almighty dollar. He was always after the next dollar and then the next one. When he came to Christ, he decided to retire. He had already made a million dollars and any more that he made he wanted to put into the Lord's work. He wanted to spend his time seeking the things of Christ.

Oh, my friend, do we put Him first? Or are we engaged in the very things that the world is engaged in and for which God intends to judge them? Well, how then can we expect that we shall escape the judgment of God? If you are in Christ, seek those things which are above, and you will not find yourself involved in the things of the world.

But now ye also put off all these; anger, wrath, malice, blasphemy, filthy communication out of your mouth [Col. 3:8].

These are the habits that we are to put off as we would put off a garment. We call a garment a habit, do we not? Many folk have a riding habit or a golfing habit. I have an old pair of slacks that I play golf in—that's my golfing habit. (I don't look very good, but that is what I wear.) Different people have different habits that they wear. Paul says that we are to put off these old practices as we'd put off a dirty, filthy garment. You don't send it to the laundry—you throw it away! You put it in the garbage can. You "put off all these."

The first is "anger." There is a place for anger that is justified. You remember that the Lord Jesus was angry at the Pharisees because of the hardness of their hearts. That is not a sinful anger. The problem is that we become angry over the wrong things.

Anger becomes "wrath" when we develop an unforgiving spirit.

Someone has said that "malice" is congealed anger. It is an anger that has been nursed along. It is an anger that tries to take revenge and get even. Paul says that a Christian is to put that off like an old, dirty, filthy garment. That kind of behavior does not represent Christ.

"Blasphemy" can be of two kinds. There is a blasphemy against God and a blasphemy against man. The first type of blasphemy is to defame the name of God. It is not just taking His name in vain, but it is to misrepresent Him, to hate Him. I received a letter from a lady that tells about the death of her little three-year-old child and how she *hated* God because of that. Somebody gave her our little booklet, *The Death of a Little Child*, and she was brought to the Lord. She realized that she had been only a church member before and had not really been born again. You see that hating God for something that has happened is really blasphemy.

Did you know that you can also blaspheme another Christian when you make a statement about him that is not true? I remember years ago a statement that was made by a man about a preacher who was Arminian in his theology. The man who made the statement was a Calvinist, and he said that the preacher was "of Satan." Well, my friend, when you say things like that, untrue things about a child of God, you are guilty of blasphemy.

"Filthy communication out of your mouth" means *foul* communication and includes both that which is abusive and that which is filthy. I can't believe that Christians would want to indulge in that, but I am told that there are certain little groups which meet together and share dirty jokes. Some Christians use swear words. In fact, I have heard of Christian leaders doing that. I do not believe that you can be a child of God, friend, and live like that. These are things that are to be put off.

Lie not one to another, seeing that ye have put off the old man with his deeds [Col. 3:9].

To whom is Paul speaking? He is writing this to believers, because he says, "seeing that ye have put off the old man with his deeds." Is it possible for a Christian to lie? It certainly is. That doesn't mean that you have lost your salvation when you do—otherwise many of us would have lost ours a long time ago. It does reveal that you don't reach a place of perfection, my friend, nor do you get rid of the old nature, when you become a child of God.

I believe one of the first sins a little child commits is to lie. I heard the story about the little boy who came running into the house and said, "Mama, Mama, a lion just ran across our front lawn." The mother said, "Willie, you *know* that was not a lion. That was a big dog that ran across the lawn. You go upstairs and confess to the Lord that you lied about that." Little Willie went upstairs and after a while he came down again. His mother asked, "Did you confess your lie to the Lord?" He answered, "Yes, I did. But the Lord said when He first saw him, He thought he was a lion, too!" Lying is something that is deep-rooted in the human heart, and many Christians still indulge in it.

And have put on the new man, which is renewed in knowledge after the image of him that created him [Col. 3:10].

"Put on the new man." If you take off the old garment, the old man, you put on the new garment, the new man. Nature abhors a vacuum. Putting off is not enough, we must live in the new man by the power of the Holy Spirit.

You and I have an old nature which has controlled us for so long that we have set up certain habits. That is why *garment* is such an effective term here—it's a habit. We have developed certain patterns in the way we say and do things. We also have within us a complex nervous system that is conditioned to respond in a set fashion. If I put my hand down on a red hot stove, a message travels through the nervous system to the brain. The message gets switched over to a motor nerve which goes back down to the hand and says, "Say, you crazy fool, take your hand off that red hot stove. You're getting burned!" And you jerk your hand off the stove. Of course, it all happens more quickly than I can tell it. It is a reflex reaction that occurs very quickly. In the same way, our habit patterns are formed.

It is psychologically true that we are able to put off old habits and form new ones. But it is especially true for the believer because he has the power of the Holy Spirit within him. We are to "put on the new man."

"Renewed in knowledge after the image of him that created him." You are to put on the new man, and that new Man is Christ. In that way the church is able to represent Him on this earth.

> **Where there is neither Greek nor Jew, circumcision nor uncircumcision, Barbarian, Scythian, bond nor free: but Christ is all, and in all [Col. 3:11].**

"Neither Greek nor Jew"—in the church, the body of believers, there is neither Greek nor Jew. This was a religious division or distinction that was made in Paul's day.

"Circumcision nor uncircumcision." This was also a religious division.

"Barbarian, Scythian." Barbarians were those who were not Greeks, those whom we would call heathen today. The Scythian was the worst kind of barbarian. Scythia was north of the Black Sea and the Caspian Sea. The people who lived there were probably the most barbaric the world has known. You talk about pagan, heathen, brutal, and mean! They would take their enemies and scalp them; then they would use the skull as a cup and drink the blood of their victims out of the skull! I cannot think of anything more heathen than that! Did you know that the ancestors of many of us who have white skin came from that territory? We are called Caucasians after the area where these barbarians lived.

Even in Paul's day, some of these people were being led to Christ. The gospel had reached out and done a tremendous work, and some of them were in the church at Colosse. Missionaries had gone north beyond the Black and Caspian Seas—Scythians had been won for Jesus

Christ. Even though they were barbarians, they were brought into that one body which is the church.

"But Christ is all, and in all." You just can't have it any more wonderful than that, my friend. This is something that is beyond description. Christ is the catalyst who brings together individuals and groups who are separate and makes them one in Him. A catalyst is a substance that is placed with elements that are opposed to each other and brings them together into a new compound. This is exactly what Christ does. We have all been made one in Him!

Remember that we are in the practical section of Colossians. In the doctrinal section we saw Christ, who is the fullness of God and the head of the church. Believers have been made full, made complete in Him. We will find all that we need in Christ, not in any man-made legal or philosophical system.

Since we have risen with Christ, we are to seek those things that are above where Christ is at the right hand of God. We have seen that this will lead to personal holiness. Beginning now with verse 12 we will find that it will also lead to *holiness in our relationship to others;* then verses 18–21 will deal with holiness in the home; and in verses 22–25 with holiness on the job. The Christian life is living out the fulness of Christ in our walk in the home, on the job, and in our social relationships.

Paul has clearly labeled the things of the old man that are to be put off. Now he will label the specifics that are to make up the wardrobe of the new man. We are going to see the latest in fashions for Christians, by the way. In fact, I have written a message on this passage of Scripture, and I have called it, "What the Well-Dressed Christian Will Wear This Year."

Put on therefore, as the elect of God, holy and beloved, bowels of mercies, kindness, humbleness of mind, meekness, longsuffering [Col. 3:12].

"The elect of God." There is a great deal of discussion about this matter of election. The fact of the matter is that if you have trusted Christ, you have on this new garment, and you are one of the elect. If these things that Paul is going to list are in your life, you're of the elect. I couldn't begin to tell you otherwise, nor argue any further about that—you're of the elect. The elect of God are clothed in the righteousness of Jesus Christ.

You will notice that the garments Paul is mentioning here are actually the fruit of the Holy Spirit. You and I cannot produce them in our lives. The minute you and I think about the wonderful position that we have in Christ and the high calling we have in Him, we have to recognize as we look at ourselves that we are impotent. We are weak and powerless, unable to "put on" these fruits. We are in the same position as the bride in the Song of Solomon. She had been kissed with the kiss of peace. Peace has been made with God. He has kissed us, my friend, and told us that our sins are forgiven us in Christ. How wonderful that is! But as the children of God we still sin. Then we need to remember the boy who got away from his father and his home, who lived in sin and wasted his fortune in riotous living. When he came back home, his father saw him afar off and ran and fell on his neck. What did he do? He kissed his son. That is the kiss of pardon, the kiss of forgiveness which God gives to His children.

We are in the position of the bride who says in the Song of Solomon, "Draw me, draw me" (see Song 1:4). I am not able to attain to this wonderful position that I have in Christ. I can't do it myself. So you and I find ourselves cast upon Him. This is where the Spirit of God moves in and enables us to walk in the Spirit.

Bowels of mercies means "heart of compassion." How heartless this world is today. How indifferent and mechanical it has become! I find that much of the time I am simply a number. In the few business transactions that I have, a computer—a machine—does business with me. I can't tell that machine how I feel. I can't tell that machine when it has made a mistake. I can't tell that machine when I have made a mistake. I just do business with that machine. It sends me a bill and I pay it—that's all. I also do business with a bank. It has as much heart as the computer. In fact, the computer *is* the heart of the bank. Since I have had cancer I must also do business with my doctor. I have a very wonderful doctor who takes care of me, but when I had to be taken to the emergency room and had a strange doctor, I found that he considered me just a boy with a stomachache. I wasn't a person to him at all. He just talked in big medical terms—that's all I was to him.

Paul is saying that as believers we should have a heart of compassion in our relationships with those around us.

Kindness is a word that Paul uses that carries with it the thought of being "profitable." It means to be helpful to others. There is another Greek word for kindness that has an element of sternness in it. You can be kind and still be stern, as when I tell my grandson, "Don't you do that." When I say that, I mean to be stern with him. But there is the kindness that means gentleness, and that is the word that Paul uses here.

Humbleness is "meekness." As I say so often, meekness does not mean weakness. Notice that here Paul's emphasis is "humbleness of mind."

Meekness. Here the emphasis is meekness of spirit.

Longsuffering is the Greek word makrothumia, which means "long-burning"—it burns a long time. We shouldn't have a short fuse with our friends and Christian brethren. We shouldn't make snap judgments.

Forbearing one another, and forgiving one another, if any man have a quarrel against any: even as Christ forgave you, so also do ye [Col. 3:13].

Quarrel actually is "complaint." Paul is including situations where there is blame involved and the complaint is justified.

What are we to do in such circumstances? "Even as Christ forgave you, so also do ye." This does not mean that you become a doormat. But it does mean that when we have a complaint, we're to go to the individual and try to work out the matter.

There are always going to be some people with whom you cannot work out things—we must realize that. When our Lord denounced the Pharisees, there was no mention of forgiveness—He just denounced them. They did not seek His forgiveness, of course.

Paul's thought here is that Christ has forgiven us so much that it won't hurt us to forgive somebody who has stepped on our toes. We are to forgive others in the same way that Christ has forgiven us.

> **And above all these things put on charity, which is the bond of perfectness.**
>
> **And let the peace of God rule in your hearts, to the which also ye are called in one body; and be ye thankful [Col. 3:14–15].**

Charity is "love." Put on love. We have here in these verses two fruits of the Spirit: love and peace.

Rule means "to umpire." The peace of God should govern our hearts.

> **Let the word of Christ dwell in you richly in all wisdom; teaching and admonishing one another in psalms and hymns and spiritual songs, singing with grace in your hearts to the Lord [Col. 3:16].**

There are many people who are great on doctrine and want to be fundamental in the faith. That is all-important, and I don't think anyone emphasizes it any more than I do. These people can often be heard praising Bible study, yet they do not attend Bible study, and they know so little about the Word of God.

"The word of Christ." The Lord Jesus said, "Now ye are clean through the word which I have spoken unto you" (John 15:3). The best Saturday night bath that you can take is to study the Word of God.

Dwell means "to be at home, to be given the run of the house." We should be familiar with the Word of God. The Bible should not be a strange book to you as it is to so many people today.

"Let the peace of God rule in your hearts"—let it be an umpire. And then "let the word of Christ *dwell* in you richly in all wisdom"—let it be at home. Know Him. Be familiar with the Word of Christ; study it and know what He's saying to you. That is where He is going to speak to you today, my friend—in His Word.

"Teaching and admonishing one another"—in what? "In psalms and hymns and spiritual songs."

"Singing with grace in your hearts to the Lord." I can't sing—so my singing never does get beyond that which is in the heart. The point is that we are to let the Word of God have this marvelous influence in our lives that Paul has described here.

And whatsoever ye do in word or deed, do all in the name of the Lord Jesus, giving thanks to God and the Father by him [Col. 3:17].

Do you want a norm for Christian conduct? Do you want a standard to go by? Do you want a principle rather than a lot of little rules? Paul gives us such a principle here. He does not say what we should or should not do. He simply says, "Do all in the name of the Lord Jesus, giving thanks to God and the Father by him." My friend, whatever you do—at your place of employment, in your home, and in all relationships with others—can you say, "I'm doing this in the name of the Lord Jesus"? If you can say that, if you are doing it in His name, then go ahead and do it. This is a marvelous standard, a yardstick that we can put down on our lives.

Now Paul comes to the subject of *holiness in the home.* You will notice that he is dealing with the same things that he dealt with in the Epistle to the Ephesians. There he told them to be filled with the Holy Spirit, and then he gave them these same instructions. Here in Colossians he writes, "Let the word of Christ dwell in you richly in all wisdom," and then he goes on to give instructions for living.

What does it mean to be filled with the Holy Spirit? It means that you will have to be filled with the Word of Christ also. The Word of God is inspired by the Spirit of God. If the Word of God dwells in you richly, then you are filled with the Spirit of God. I do not believe that you can be filled with the Holy Spirit or that you can serve Christ until you are filled with the knowledge of His Word. "Let the word of Christ dwell in you richly."

Now, if the Word of Christ dwells in your richly, it will work itself out in your life, and it will have an effect on your home.

Wives, submit yourselves unto your own husbands, as it is fit in the Lord [Col. 3:18].

This is for the purpose of order in the home. This is not for the purpose of producing a browbeating husband. I do not believe that God intends for a wife to submit to an unsaved husband who beats her or orders her to do things contrary to her walk with the Lord.

A woman wrote to me and said that her husband was an unsaved man. When he would get drunk, he would beat her. She felt as a Christian she ought to stay with him. I advised her to leave him. I do not believe that God ever asks any woman to stay with a drunken husband. She loses her own personality; she loses her own dignity, and she will find herself being brought down to his level if she submits to that. She is to submit "as it is fit in the Lord."

Husbands, love your wives, and be not bitter against them [Col. 3:19].

The husband who loves his wife is the one to whom the wife is to submit. She is not to be the one to take the lead in the family, but she is to urge him to take the lead. I think we have had this thing all wrong for a long time. In my entire ministry I have removed the word *obey* from the marriage ceremony. I don't think it belongs in there at all.

Children, obey your parents in all things: for this is well pleasing unto the Lord [Col. 3:20].

Children are to obey their parents. They are to honor their parents all their lives, but when they are children they are to obey them.

However, the child also needs to grow up. I don't think this verse means that a twenty-four-year-old boy must stay tied to his mama's apron strings. Whether he is married or single, when he has reached maturity, he is ready to get away from his parents. We see so many teenagers rebelling against their parents in our day. I believe that God may have put into the hearts of teenagers the necessity to get away. There is a period in their lives that is a weaning time, and they need to learn to be independent. I have seen some literature that tells young married couples that they are still to go to their parents and obey them. I think that is nonsense and entirely unscriptural (see Gen. 2:24). "Children, obey your parents in all things" is a verse for children, for minors.

Fathers, provoke not your children to anger, lest they be discouraged [Col. 3:21].

Let me refer you to my book on Ephesians and my comment on Ephesians 6:4. The remarkable feature of this verse, as given both in Ephesians and Colossians, is that under the Mosaic Law, the commandment referred only to the children. There was no reference to parents. Had the Law developed in the parents a dictatorship rather than a directorship? No. The Book of Proverbs reveals that the responsibility to find God's will for the child had been given to the parents: "Train up a child in the way he should go: and when he is old, he will not depart from it" (Prov. 22:6).

Now the apostle moves on to the subject of *holiness on the job*, at the place of employment. He will discuss the relationships that exist on the job, the relationship of capital to labor.

Servants, obey in all things your masters according to the flesh; not with eye-service, as men-pleasers; but in singleness of heart, fearing God [Col. 3:22].

Eye-service is a word peculiar in the New Testament to the writings of Paul. He means, "Don't keep your eye on the clock. Keep your eye on Christ. He is the One whom you are serving." That is the way you ought to do your job.

Sometimes Christians talk about being dedicated to the Lord and wanting to serve the Lord, but they are lazy. We had one boy working here at our radio headquarters who was like that. He stood around with his hands in his pockets all the while his mouth was going, but he thought he was dedicated! May I say something very frankly? If you are lazy on the job, you are *not* dedicated to Jesus Christ.

Paul had reduced the Christian life to its lowest common denominator. He had one simple goal: ". . . forgetting those things which are behind, and reaching forth unto those things which are before, I press toward the mark for the prize of the high calling of God in Christ Jesus" (Phil. 3:13–14). He had his eye, his mind, his heart, and his total affections fixed upon Jesus Christ.

"In singleness of heart, fearing God." The idea here is not to fear the boss, but to fear God

And whatsoever ye do, do it heartily, as to the Lord, and not unto men [Col. 3:23].

When Paul says to work "heartily," he means work from your soul. We have heard a lot about a "soul brother," but we ought to have a little more "soul work." If you can't do something with enthusiasm unto the Lord, regardless of what it is, it is wrong for you. Some people write in and ask me, "Is it right for me to do this?" or "Is it right for me to go to this place?" Here is your standard: "Whatsoever ye do, do it heartily, as to the Lord." That applies to everything. Even if you cannot go to a church with enthusiasm, I would recommend you quit going to that church.

"As to the Lord, and not unto men." Whatever we do should be done to the Lord, not to men. We are not to be men pleasers.

Knowing that of the Lord ye shall receive the reward of the inheritance: for ye serve the Lord Christ [Col. 3:24].

Maybe you're not going to have to report to your boss; or when his back is turned he doesn't see that you are loafing on the job, not really giving him a full day's work. But the Lord Jesus sees, and you are going to answer to Him. You are in Him, and you belong to Him. Therefore, you have to give an account of your life to Him.

Since we represent the Lord Jesus down here upon this earth, He is going to ask that His representatives be found faithful. There are a great many folk who are humble, little-known people that you and I know nothing about who have been *faithful* on the job. They have been faithful to their employer, faithful to their church, faithful to their homes, faithful to their pastor. Very few people know about them. The Lord knows. They will receive a reward. I think you and I are going to be surprised by the reward some people will get.

"For ye serve the Lord Christ." This puts a different complexion upon Christian service down here. There are many people who are lazy in God's work. I would say that laziness is one of the curses of the ministry. It is found in the church staff. It is so easy to loaf on the job because nobody is looking, nobody is watching. We need to remember that we serve the Lord Jesus, and we are going to give an account to Him.

> **But he that doeth wrong shall receive for the wrong which he hath done: and there is no respect of persons [Col. 3:25].**

He is going to straighten out everything in your life and in my life that we don't straighten out down here. This is exactly what this means.

It is a privilege to be in God's service. It is a privilege to teach a Sunday school class. But don't ever think that this makes you something special. When the Lord judges you, He will judge you on *faithfulness*. All will be judged alike. God is no respecter of persons.

My friend, we are joined to a living Christ. How wonderful it is! I cannot attain to it in my own strength. But He says He is going to help me. Only the Holy Spirit working in me can attain this high and holy calling. He wants me to mirror Him in every relationship I have down here. What a glorious calling you and I have! Doesn't that give you enthusiasm today? Don't look to the Babe in Bethlehem. Go to the living Christ who is at God's right hand.

CHAPTER 4

THEME: Fellowship of believers is hearty

We are in the section of this epistle which is dealing with holiness on the job, at the place of employment. Chapter 3 concluded with exhortations to servants or to employees. Chapter 4 will continue with exhortations to masters or to employers.

> **Masters, give unto your servants that which is just and equal; knowing that ye also have a Master in heaven [Col. 4:1].**

"Masters"—Paul has something to say not only to the servant but also to the masters, to the bosses.

"Equal" means not to level down but to level up. The master is to do right by his servant.

"Knowing that ye also have a Master in heaven." The master will stand before Christ someday. Every Christian employer, as well as employee, will stand before God. This does put the gospel in shoe leather, does it not? It gets right down where the rubber meets the road. Or, in this case, it gets right down where your foot is walking in the factory or in the office. Whatever you're doing, you are to do it unto the Lord, because you are going to answer to Him if you are His child.

Now the next few verses present three more areas of Christian conduct which are important. They are prayer, our public walk, and speech.

> **Continue in prayer, and watch in the same with thanksgiving [Col. 4:2].**

These two words go together: Pray and watch. They are very important. They remind us of the experience of Nehemiah. When the enemy tried to stop him from rebuilding the walls of Jerusalem, he didn't just throw in the towel and cry out that he couldn't do the job. Nor did he simply say, "Well, we'll make it a matter of prayer," and then go on as he had been. No, this is what Nehemiah said: "Nevertheless we made our prayer unto our God, and set a watch against them day and night, because of them" (Neh. 4:9). This is what Paul tells us here: Watch and pray.

An old pastor in Georgia used to make this statement: "When a farmer prays for a corn crop, God expects him to say 'Amen' with a hoe." If you are praying about a certain matter, get busy with it.

I'm afraid we hear a lot of pious nonsense about prayer. I received a letter from a preacher who has cancer. He said, "I've been to Mayo Clinic. They found that I have cancer, and they recommend an operation. But I have come home and decided that I would do like you did: I will just trust the Lord." I sat down and wrote him a letter in a hurry. I said, "Brother, I did trust the Lord but that wasn't all that I did. I went to whom I think is the finest cancer specialist out here on the West Coast. My case was brought up before the UCLA Medical Clinic and was discussed there. They recommended the best thing that medical science knew to do. I have had two operations for cancer. My Christian brother, if you want to be an intelligent Christian (and I think you are), then you go back to Mayo Clinic as quickly as you can and tell them to operate if that is what they think is best. Then you trust the Lord, and He will bring you through it. *That* is what I did." Watch and pray. Be on the job. This is so practical.

"With thanksgiving." Be sure and thank God always because He is going to hear and answer your prayer. Maybe it won't be the answer you wanted, but He will answer. This is like breathing: inhale by prayer, exhale by thanksgiving.

> **Withal praying also for us, that God would open unto us a door of utterance, to speak the mystery of Christ, for which I am also in bonds:**
>
> **That I may make it manifest, as I ought to speak [Col. 4:3–4].**

"Withal praying also for us"—Paul says, "Don't forget to pray for us." My friend, you can't help Paul any longer by praying for him, but you can help your pastor and other Christian ministries.

"That God would open unto us a door of utterance, to speak the mystery of Christ, for which I am also in bonds." Paul was in prison when he wrote this. He wanted to be released and go out through an open door that he might preach the gospel.

I consider every aspect of my ministry to be a door, and I ask God to keep the doors open. He has promised that He would. This is the verse that I have chosen for my ministry: ". . . behold, I have set before thee an open door, and no man can shut it: for thou hast a little strength, and hast kept my word, and hast not denied my name" (Rev. 3:8). He has set a lot of open doors before me, and I ask Him to open even more doors.

> **Walk in wisdom toward them that are without, redeeming the time [Col. 4:5].**

"Walk in wisdom." The child of God has a responsibility before the world today. Don't be foolish as a child of God.

We hear so much pious nonsense in our day. There are those who said the Lord would return by 1980. I don't know where they got such information. There were probably a lot of embarrassed folk with red faces in 1980. Christians have no right to make such statements before an unsaved world. Nor should we say we are trusting the Lord when our actions show that we really are not trusting Him. We should not do foolish things before the world.

A woman in Southern California wrote me a letter and rebuked me for going to the doctor for treatment of my cancer. She said that that was not trusting the Lord. She wrote, "I have cancer and I am trusting the Lord. I don't go to the doctor." They buried her not long ago; she died of her cancer. I'm afraid at times we are guilty of causing our neighbors to smile and say, "This Christianity is a foolish sort of thing." We need to learn to "walk in wisdom toward them that are without."

"Redeeming the time." Buy up your opportunities. When you see an opportunity, pray that the Lord will lead you. Don't force yourself on people. Just pray and ask the Lord to open the door, and He will open it. I wish I had space to tell you how many times this has happened in my life and in the lives of others. Let Him open the door—before you make the mistake of putting your foot in your mouth. I knocked on many doors when I was a pastor, and I often stepped in and put my foot in my mouth the very first thing. Since then I have learned to do a lot more praying before I walk in.

Let your speech be alway with grace, seasoned with salt, that ye may know how ye ought to answer every man [Col. 4:6].

Some people think this verse says, "Let your speech be salt," and they really sting you with their little sarcastic remarks! But what it says is, "always with grace, seasoned with salt." A child of God should have a conversation that deters evil. It should withhold evil rather than promote it. I think it also means that a Christian should not be boring. We should be enthusiastic—"That ye may know how ye ought to answer every man."

FELLOWSHIP OF BELIEVERS IS HEARTY

We come now to a remarkable list of names of people whom Paul knew. They are men and women who lived back there in the first century. They walked down the Roman roads, lived in Roman cities, and were under Roman rule. They were in the midst of paganism, but they were God's children.

Many of these people lived in Ephesus. When I was in Ephesus, I climbed up in the theater there and from that height I could look down that great marble boulevard—I would call it Harbor Boulevard, because it leads right down to where the harbor was in that day. I thought, *This is where one could have seen Paul come walking up the boulevard. There would be Tychicus coming up the way; and there's*

Onesimus and Aristarchus and Epaphras—all those fellows. They were all Christians. They were God's men back yonder in the first century.

The interesting thing is that Paul had never been to Rome nor had he been to Colosse, yet he gives a list of people that he knew, and many of them are from those two cities. This reveals that Paul had led many people to Christ who returned home to cities that he never was able to reach directly or personally. His ministry was a tremendous, far-reaching ministry.

> **All my state shall Tychicus declare unto you, who is a beloved brother, and a faithful minister and fellow-servant in the Lord:**
>
> **Whom I have sent unto you for the same purpose, that he might know your estate, and comfort your hearts [Col. 4:7–8].**

"Tychicus" was the pastor of the church in Ephesus. He is mentioned in Ephesians 6:21, Acts 20:4, and 2 Timothy 4:12. He was a wonderful brother in the Lord.

> **With Onesimus, a faithful and beloved brother, who is one of you. They shall make known unto you all things which are done here [Col. 4:9].**

"Onesimus" was a slave of Philemon in Colosse. He had run away from his master, had been led to the Lord through the ministry of Paul, and was now being sent back to his master by him. Paul wrote a letter to Philemon when he sent Onesimus back, and he tells Philemon that Onesimus is his "beloved brother." You can see from this that there is a new relationship in Christ. Master and slave are now brothers in Christ Jesus.

> **Aristarchus my fellow-prisoner saluteth you, and Marcus, sister's son to Barnabas, (touching whom ye re-**

ceived commandments: if he come unto you, receive
him;) [Col. 4:10].

"Aristarchus" was a fellow prisoner with Paul, and he was his friend.

"Marcus" is John Mark, the nephew of Barnabas—the son of his
sister. He is the writer of the Gospel of Mark. You will remember that
Mark left Paul and Barnabas on their first missionary journey, and because of this Paul didn't want to take him along on the second missionary journey. Paul was wrong in his judgment of John Mark. The
boy made good, and Paul acknowledges that here. Paul gives the Colossians instructions, "Don't reject him like I did. You folks receive
him." Paul mentions John Mark again in his second letter to Timothy:
". . . Take Mark, and bring him with thee: for he is profitable to me for
the ministry" (2 Tim. 4:11).

And Jesus, which is called Justus, who are of the circumcision. These only are my fellow-workers unto the
kingdom of God, which have been a comfort unto me
[Col. 4:11].

"Jesus, which is called Justus" would be the name *Joshua* in the Hebrew language. Being "of the circumcision" indicates he was Jewish.
This shows us that there were a few Israelites in the church in Colosse.
However, there were not many; the Colossian church was mostly Gentile. These men were wonderful brethren, helpers of Paul, and great
missionaries themselves.

Epaphras, who is one of you, a servant of Christ, salut-
eth you, always labouring fervently for you in prayers,
that ye may stand perfect and complete in all the will of
God [Col. 4:12].

"Epaphras" was the pastor in Colosse. Now he is in prison, so he has a
new ministry, the ministry of prayer. I received a letter from a young
preacher who is paralyzed and cannot preach any more. He wrote a
most discouraged letter. I answered him like this: "I have a job for

you: Pray for me." Prayer is a ministry, too. If God takes you out of active service, pray for God's servants. It simply means God has given you a new ministry; He has something different for you to do.

> **For I bear him record, that he hath a great zeal for you, and them that are in Laodicea, and them in Hierapolis [Col. 4:13].**

These three cities were very close together. Hierapolis and Laodicea were about six to ten miles apart; they were both near Colosse. There were churches in all three places.

> **Luke, the beloved physician, and Demas, greet you [Col. 4:14].**

"Luke, the beloved physician." Isn't that a wonderful designation for him?

When Paul first mentioned Demas, he called him a fellow worker. Here he simply says, "and Demas"; I think this may indicate that Paul isn't really sure about him at this time. Later on Demas will forsake Paul. How tragic that is.

> **Salute the brethren which are in Laodicea, and Nymphas, and the church which is in his house [Col. 4:15].**

These cities had great heathen temples, but the Christians met in homes. I used to hold the viewpoint and I still do—although I don't emphasize it today as I did at one time—that as the church started in the home, it is going to come back to the home.

> **And when this epistle is read among you, cause that it be read also in the church of the Laodiceans; and that ye likewise read the epistle from Laodicea [Col. 4:16].**

"The epistle from Laodicea." Paul does not say that he had written an epistle *to* the Laodiceans. Apparently the letters of Paul were circulated around, and the Laodiceans had read one of them. A great many of the scholars believe that this might be a reference to the Epistle to the Ephesians. Paul is telling the Colossians to read that epistle also and to share theirs with the Laodiceans.

> **And say to Archippus, Take heed to the ministry which thou hast received in the Lord, that thou fulfil it [Col. 4:17].**

"Archippus" is another man on Paul's list in this letter. We do not know anything more about him than is mentioned here. He is a man who had a gift, and Paul is urging him to use that gift.

> **The salutation by the hand of me Paul. Remember my bonds. Grace be with you. Amen [Col. 4:18].**

Paul dictated most of his letters. (The letter to the Galatians was written in his own hand.) Here he gives his signature to the letter which he has dictated.

This is the second time that Paul says, "Remember my bonds"—or, "Pray for me."

"Grace be with you. Amen." Isn't this a wonderful letter that we have read? Paul wrote to a church that he had never visited, but he knew many of the people and had led them to the knowledge of the Lord Jesus Christ.

BIBLIOGRAPHY

(Recommended for Further Study)

Gromacki, Robert G. *Stand Perfect in Wisdom: An Exposition of Colossians and Philemon*. Grand Rapids, Michigan: Baker Book House, 1981.

Harrison, Everett F. *Colossians: Christ-All-Sufficient*. Chicago, Illinois: Moody Press, 1971.

Hendriksen, William. *Exposition of Colossians and Philemon*. Grand Rapids, Michigan: Baker Book House, 1965.

Ironside, H. A. *Lectures on the Epistle to the Colossians*. Neptune, New Jersey: Loizeaux Brothers, 1929.

Kelly, William. *Lectures on the Epistles to the Philippians and Colossians*. Oak Park, Illinois: Bible Truth Publishers, n.d.

Kent, Homer A., Jr. *Treasures of Wisdom: Studies in Colossians and Philemon*. Grand Rapids, Michigan: Baker Book House, 1978. (Excellent.)

King, Guy H. *Crossing the Border*. Fort Washington, Pennsylvania: Christian Literature Crusade, 1957. (Devotional.)

Moule, Handley C. G. *Colossians and Philemon*. Grand Rapids, Michigan: Kregel Publications, 1893. (This is a reprint from *The Cambridge University Bible for Schools and Colleges*. This helpful series also covers Romans, Ephesians, and Philippians.)

Nicholson, William. *Oneness with Christ*. Grand Rapids, Michigan: Kregel Publications, 1903. (Devotional.)

Robertson, A. T. *Paul and the Intellectuals*. Grand Rapids, Michigan: Baker Book House, 1928.

Thomas, W. H. Griffith. *Studies in Colossians and Philemon*. Grand Rapids, Michigan: Baker Book House, 1973. (Excellent.)

Vaughan, Curtis. *Colossians and Philemon: A Study Guide*. Grand Rapids, Michigan: Zondervan Publishing House, 1980.

Vine, W. E. *Philippians and Colossians*. London: Oliphants, 1955. (This is an excellent treatment.)

Wiersbe, Warren W. *Be Complete*. Wheaton, Illinois: Victor Books, 1981.

Wuest, Kenneth S. *Ephesians and Colossians in the Greek New Testament*. Grand Rapids, Michigan: Wm. B. Eerdmans Publishing Co., 1953.